Knitted Icons

ISBN 978-1-59474-209-5

Library of Congress Cataloging in Publication Number: 2007928851

First published in the United Kingdom in 2007 by
Collins & Brown
10 Southcombe Street
London
W14 0RA

An imprint of Anova Books Company Ltd

Commissioning Editor: Michelle Lo
Designer Manager: Gemma Wilson
Photographer: Michael Wicks
Designer: Jeremy Tilston
Assistant Editor: Katie Hudson
Illustrator: Kang Chen
Senior Production Controller: Morna McPherson

Reproduction by Spectrum Colour, Ipswich
Printed and bound by Craft Print International Ltd, Singapore

Distributed in North America by Chronicle Books
680 Second Street
San Francisco, CA 94107

10 9 8 7 6 5 4 3 2 1

Quirk Books
215 Church Street
Philadelphia, PA 19106
www.quirkbooks.com

Knitted Icons

25 Celebrity Doll Patterns

QUIRK BOOKS
PHILADELPHIA

Contents

Introduction 7
Knit Basics 8
Sewing Basics 15
Basic Doll 18
Marilyn Monroe 20
Bruce Lee 24
Abraham Lincoln 28
Jackie O 30
Che Guevara 34
Jimi Hendrix 36
Albert Einstein 39
Cher 42
James Dean 46
Muhammad Ali 49
King Kong 52
Godzilla 55
Madonna 58
Andy Warhol 63
Chairman Mao 66
The Beatles 68
Charlie Chaplin 73
Gandhi 76
Queen Elizabeth II 78
Bob Marley 81
Audrey Hepburn 84
Bob Dylan 87
Mr T 90
David Bowie 93
Elvis 96
Templates 100
Techniques and Abbreviations/Resources 112

Introduction

When I first embarked upon this project I had no idea just how much fun I was getting myself into. Bringing each character to life was a challenge: assessing who they were as characters and personalities and amplifying the best they had to offer. The first step was researching all the characters—from Andy Warhol's Studio 57 to Cher's latest CD and Godzilla in Tokyo...in a matter of moments, my world became engulfed in twentieth-century pop culture.

I've designed this book to be used by beginner and experienced knitters. I've included instructions for all basic knitting and sewing techniques to make the stitch process a breeze. Once you've mastered the basics, then you're ready to create your own doll. From James Dean to Audrey Hepburn, Marilyn Monroe to Jimi Hendrix, knitting these dolls can be as addictive as their personalities.

Fun photographs and step-by-step instructions accompany each project, and I have costumes suited to knitters/sewers/fanatics of all skill levels—with simple patterns such as Bruce Lee's pants for the knitting novice to more complicated projects like Elvis's infamous white jumpsuit. The materials used have been chosen to ensure maximum impact, though you could easily substitute and add your own creative touches.

You will be amazed at how quickly and easily the characters start to come to life. Whether you are looking for Madonna's "blonde ambition" or Elvis's curling lip and signature quiff, pick up your needles and have a go—there's an icon for everyone.

Carol Meldrum

KNIT BASICS

The following steps provide you with everything you need to create your very own knitted icon. It's easier than you think!

WORKING FROM A PATTERN

Before starting any pattern, always read it through. This will give you an idea of how the design is structured and the techniques that are involved. Each pattern includes the following basic elements:

Materials

This section gives a list of materials required, including the amount of yarn, sizes of needles, and any buttons or zippers. The yarn amounts specified are based on average requirements and are therefore approximate.

Abbreviations

Knitting instructions are normally given in an abbreviated form, which saves valuable space. In this book the most commonly used abbreviations are listed on page 112 and additional abbreviations specific to a project are listed on the project page.

Project instructions

Before starting to knit, read the instructions carefully to understand the abbreviations used, how the design is structured, and in which order each piece is worked. However, there may be some parts of the pattern that only become clear when you are knitting them, so do not assume that you are being slow or that the pattern is wrong. Asterisks or brackets are used to indicate the repetition of a sequence of stitches. For example: *k3, P1; rep from * to end. This means, knit three stitches, then purl one stitch, then repeat this sequence to the end of the row. It could also be written: [k3, P1] to end. Asterisks and brackets may be used together in a row. For example: *k4, P1, [k1, P1] 3 times; rep from * to end. The part of the instruction in brackets indicates that these stitches only are to be repeated three times before returning to the instructions immediately after the asterisk.

When repeating anything, make sure that you are doing so the correct number of times. For example: [k1, P1] twice means that 4 stitches are worked, but *k1, P1; rep from * twice more means 6 stitches are worked. The phrase "work even" means continue without increasing or decreasing the number of stitches and keeping the established pattern correct.

When you put your knitting aside, always mark where you are on the pattern; it is better to be safe than sorry, especially if a complex stitch is involved.

If the numeral 0 appears within an instruction, for example, "k1(0,1,2) sts," this means that for that particular size no stitches are worked at that point. Take special care if the sizes have been separated for a particular instruction. For example, suppose that the pattern states "First and 4th sizes only: Bind off 15 (20) sts, work to end." For the first size, follow the instructions

outside the parentheses, and for the 4th size follow those within them. For any other size, these instructions do not apply.

Gauge (tension) and selecting correct needle size

Gauge (tension) can differ quite dramatically between knitters. This is because of the way that the needles and the yarn are held. So if your gauge (tension) does not match that stated in the pattern, you should change your needle size following this simple rule:

- If your knitting is too loose, your gauge (tension) will read that you have fewer stitches and rows than the given gauge (tension), and you

will need to change to a smaller needle to make the stitch size smaller.

- If your knitting is too tight, your gauge (tension) will read that you have more stitches and rows than the given gauge (tension), and you will need to change to a thicker needle to make the stitch size bigger.

Finishing

The Finishing section in each project will tell you how to join the knitted pieces together. Always follow the recommended sequence.

Always take the time to check your gauge—it ensures the accuracy of your knitting!

KNITTING A GAUGE SWATCH

No matter how excited you are about a new knitting project and how annoying it seems to have to spend time knitting a gauge swatch before you start, please do take the time, as it will not be wasted.

Use the same needles, yarn, and stitch pattern as those that will be used for the main work and knit a sample at least 5in (12.5cm) square. Smooth out

the finished piece on a flat surface, but do not stretch it.

To check the stitch gauge, place a ruler horizontally on the sample, measure 4in (10cm) across, and mark with a pin at each end. Count the number of stitches between the pins. To check the row gauge, place a ruler vertically on the sample, measure 4in

(10cm), and mark with pins. Count the number of rows between the pins. If the number of stitches and rows is greater then specified in the pattern, make a new swatch using larger needles; if it is less, make a new swatch using smaller needles.

MAKING A SLIPKNOT

A slipknot is the basis of all casting-on techniques and is therefore the starting point for almost everything you do in knitting.

1 Wind the yarn around two fingers twice as shown. Insert a knitting needle through the first (front) strand and under the second (back) one.

2 Using the needle, pull the back strand through the front one to form a loop. Holding the loose ends of the yarn with your left hand, pull the needle upward, thus tightening the knot.

CASTING ON

Casting on is the term used for making a row of stitches to be used as a foundation for your knitting.

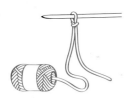  

1 Hold the needle in your right hand with the ball end of the yarn over your index finger. Wind the loose end of the yarn around your left thumb from front to back.

2 Insert the point of the needle under the first strand of yarn on your thumb.

3 With your right index finger, take the ball end of the yarn over the point of the needle.

4 Pull a loop through to form the first stitch. Remove your left thumb from the yarn. Pull the loose end to secure the stitch. Rep from * until required number of sts have been cast on.

THE BASIC STITCHES

The knit and purl stitches form the basis of all knitted fabrics. The knit stitch is the easiest to learn, and once you have mastered this you can move on to the purl stitch.

Knit Stitch

1 Hold the needle with the cast-on stitches in your left hand, with the loose yarn at the back of the work. Insert the right-hand needle from left to right through the front of the first stitch on the left-hand needle.

2 Wrap the yarn from left to right over the point of the right-hand needle.

3 Draw the yarn through the stitch, thus forming a new stitch on the right-hand needle.

4 Slip the original stitch off the left-hand needle, keeping the new stitch on the right-hand needle. To knit a row, repeat steps 1 to 4 until all the stitches have been transferred from the left-hand needle to the right-hand needle.

Use a pair of needles that is one size larger to cast on so that the cast-on row isn't tight when knitting the first row.

Purl Stitch

Soda can rings make great cost-effective markers for knitting!

1 Hold the needle with the stitches in your left hand, with the loose yarn at the front of the work. Insert the right-hand needle from right to left into the front of the first stitch on the left-hand needle.

2 Wrap the yarn from right to left, up and over the point of the right-hand needle.

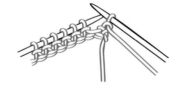

3 Draw the yarn through the stitch, thus forming a new stitch on the right-hand needle.

4 Slip the original stitch off the left-hand needle, keeping the new stitch on the right-hand needle. To purl a row, repeat steps 1–4 until all the stitches have been transferred from the left-hand needle to the right-hand needle.

INCREASING AND DECREASING

Many projects will require some shaping, either just to add interest or to allow them to fit comfortably. Shaping is achieved by increasing or decreasing the number of stitches you are working.

Increasing

The simplest method of increasing one stitch is to work into the front and back of the same stitch. On a knit row, knit into the front of the stitch to be increased into, then before slipping it off the needle, place the right-hand needle behind the left-hand one and knit again into the back of it (inc). Slip the original stitch off the left-hand needle.

On a purl row, purl into the front of the stitch to be increased into, then before slipping it off the needle, purl again into the back of it. Slip the original stitch off the left-hand needle.

Decreasing

The simplest method of decreasing one stitch is to work two stitches together. On a knit row, insert the right-hand needle from left to right through two stitches instead of one, then knit them together as one stitch. This is called knit two together (k2tog).

On a purl row, insert the right-hand needle from right to left through two stitches instead of one, then purl them together as one stitch. This is called purl two together (p2tog).

SPECIAL STITCHES

Loop stitch is a variation of double crochet and is usually worked on wrong-side rows because the loops form at the back of the fabric.

Loop (Fur) Stitch

1 Insert hook into the st below. Using a free finger, pull up the yarn to form a loop. Pick up both strands of the loop and draw through.

2 Wrap the supply yarn over the hook.

3 Draw the yarn through all 3 loops. **NOTE:** When each loop is cut afterward, the texture of the fabric resembles fur.

Making a Stitch

Another form of increasing involves working into the strand between two stitches. This is usually called "make one stitch" (m1).

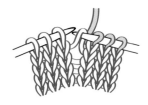 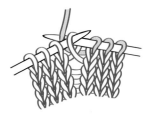 

1 Insert the right-hand needle from front to back under the horizontal strand that runs between the stitches on the right and left-hand needles.

2 Insert the left-hand needle under the strand from front to back, twisting it as shown, to prevent a hole from forming, and knit (or purl) through the back of the loop.

3 Slip the new stitch off the left-hand needle.

BINDING OFF

This is the most commonly used method of securing stitches once you have finished a piece of knitting. The bound-off edge should have the same "give" or elasticity as the fabric, and you should bind off in the stitch used for the main fabric unless the pattern directs otherwise.

Knitwise

Knit two stitches. *Using the point of the left-hand needle, lift the first stitch on the right-hand needle over the second, then drop it off the needle. Knit the next stitch and repeat from * until all stitches have been worked off the left-hand needle and only one stitch remains on the right-hand needle. Cut the yarn, leaving enough to sew in the end, thread the end through the stitch, then slip it off the needle. Draw the yarn up firmly to fasten off.

Purlwise

Purl two stitches. *Using the point of the left-hand needle, lift the first stitch on the right-hand needle over the second and drop it off the needle. Purl the next stitch and repeat from * until all the stitches have been worked off the left-hand needle and only one stitch remains on the right-hand needle. Secure the last stitch as described in binding off knitwise.

SEWING BASICS

From transferring patterns and markings to fabric to basic embroidery, these basic techniques make the sewing process a breeze.

GENERAL TECHNIQUES

Using templates

Turn to page 100 for the pattern templates for the projects. All templates have been reduced on page to 50% of their size. To enlarge them to the correct size, simply photocopy the pattern using the enlargement button on a photocopier. Photocopy all templates at 200%.

Transferring patterns and markings to fabric

For heavy fabrics and colored or patterned cottons, place carbon paper between the pattern and the wrong side of the fabric. Trace over it with a pencil or tracing wheel. Alternatively, cut out the pattern pieces and draw around them with a water-soluble fabric marker. Then mark the dots and other features with the carbon paper. Employ this method for transferring shapes for patchwork piecing.

For lightweight fabrics, trace the design using a water-soluble fabric marker. Tape the pattern piece to a window (in daylight) or a light-box. Place the fabric over it, right side up, and trace the lines on to the fabric.

To transfer dots, darts, and other placement markings to fabric, pin the pattern to the wrong side of the fabric and insert a pin at the marking. Lift up the edge of the pattern and mark the fabric with a water-soluble fabric marker.

Inserting stuffing

As with all soft toys, how you stuff your doll will directly affect the finished appearance. It is important to stuff firmly, but without stretching the knitting out of place. Always stuff down the extremities, such as the legs and arms, first and mold into shape as you go along. A pair of forceps or tweezers, or even a pencil, are very useful for stuffing. The amount of stuffing needed for each doll depends on the knitting tension and individual taste.

Inserting a zipper

Use a backstitch to sew the zipper in place. A backstitch is created by bringing the needle into the fabric behind the previous stitch.

Remember to stitch through only one layer of the fabric. Use tight, even, small stitches.

Bar tack the end of the zipper to create a very strong hold. This area of the zipper will get pulled on and must be anchored strongly.

Sewing a button

1. Thread your needle and tie a knot at the end of the thread.
2. Position the button on the fabric. Push the threaded needle up through the fabric and through one hole in the button. Pull the thread all the way up.
3. Push the needle down through the next hole and through the fabric. On a 4-hole button choose the one diagonal to the first hole if you want the threads to cross an "X." If you want two parallel lines of thread showing, choose the hole opposite the first hole. Still holding the pin in place, pull the thread all the way through. Once that is done, the pin will be kept in place by the thread.
4. Bring the needle up through the first hole (for a 2-hole button) or a new hole (for a 4-hole button) and pull the thread all the way through the fabric.
5. Repeat the sewing process enough times to make sure the button is securely in place. On the last stitch, push the needle through the material, but not through a hole in the button. Pull the thread out into the area between button and material, remove the pin and pull up the button a little, and twist the thread six times around the thread between the button and the material to reinforce the shank you have created. Then push the needle back down through the material.

Pressing seams

Set the temperature on your iron and press the seam as it was sewn. On the WS, open the body of the fabric and coax the seam open with the tip of the iron on the right side of the seam. Open the fabric and lay it as flat as possible with the seam allowance up. Use the tip of the iron to press the seam allowance open. Turn the fabric over and press the seam from the right side of the fabric. Repeat as necessary until you have a flat seam that has become part of the fabric.

Tassels

Wrap the chosen yarn several times around a piece of cardboard the same length as your desired length of tassel, until the tassel is as bulky as required. Cut another length of yarn and thread it through the top, securing with a knot. Cut through all the loops at the lower edge of the tassel, then take one end of the yarn at the top and thread it through to where you wish your tassel to be tied. Wrap the end of the length around the tassel several times and secure. Trim the ends, and the tassel is finished.

French knots

1 Come up at **A** and wrap the thread around the needle once in counter-clockwise direction.

2 Wrap the thread around the needle a second time in the same direction, keeping the needle away from the fabric.

3 Push the wraps together and slide to the end of the needle. Go down close to the start point, pulling the thread through to form a knot.

Running Stitch

Backstitch

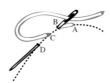

Come up at A, go down at B, then come up at C. Do not pull the thread through the fabric. Go down at D, come up at E. Pull the thread through gently, so the fabric does not pucker.

Continue following the design line as shown by repeating Steps 1 and 2. Keep stitches even.

Working from right to left, come up at A, go down at B, then come up at C. Pull the thread through.

Go down again at B to make a backstitch, then come up at D, ready for the next stitch, and continue.

Basic Doll

MATERIALS

★ Wool Cotton by Rowan, approx 122yd/50g ball (50% wool/ 50% cotton)
    1 ball in Ecru 900 (MC)
★ 1 pair of US 3 (3.25mm) needles
★ Fiberfill for stuffing
(See also specific doll patterns for additional materials for embroidery, hair, and costumes for each doll)

SIZE

Approximate height 10½in (26cm)

GAUGE

26 sts x 32 rows = 4in (10cm) square over St st using US 3 (3.25mm) needles and MC yarn

PATTERN

***Body** (make 2)*

Using US size 3 (3.25mm) needles and MC yarn, cast on 16 sts.

Row 1: Knit to end.

Row 2: Purl to end.

Row 3: K1, m1, k14, m1, k1. (18 sts)

Row 4: Purl.

Row 5: K1, m1, k16, m1, k1. (20 sts)

Row 6: Purl.

Work in St st for a further 12 rows ending with a WS row.

Next row: K1, sl1, k1, psso, k14, k2tog, k1. (18 sts)

Work 3 rows St st.

Next row: K1, sl1, k1, psso, k12, k2tog, k1. (16 sts)

Next row: P1, p2tog, p10, p2tog tbl, p1. (14 sts)

Next row: K1, sl1, k1, psso, k8, k2tog, k1. (12 sts)

Next row: Purl.

Bind off.

Head *(make 2)*

Using US size 3 (3.25mm) needles and MC yarn, cast on 12 sts.

Row 1: Knit to end.

Row 2: Purl to end.

Row 3: K1, m1, k10, m1, k1. (14 sts)

Row 4: Purl to end.

Row 5: K1, m1, k12, m1, k1. (16 sts)

Row 6: Purl to end.

Work in St st for a further 10 rows ending on a WS row.

Next row: K1, sl1, k1, psso, k10, k2tog, k1. (14 sts)

Next row: Purl to end.

Next row: K1, sl1, k1, psso, k8, k2tog, k1. (12 sts)

Next row: Purl to end.

Bind off.

Leg *(make 2)*

Using US size 3 (3.25mm) needles and MC yarn, cast on 11 sts.

Row 1: Knit to end.

Row 2: Purl to end.

Rep Rows 1–2 14 times more (28 rows more in total).

Next row: K1, m1, knit to last stitch, m1, k1. (13 sts)

Work 3 more rows in St st.

Next row: K1, m1, knit to last stitch, m1, k1. (15 sts).

Next row: Purl to end.

Bind off.

Arm *(make 2)*

Using US size 3 (3.25mm) needles and MC yarn, cast on 7 sts.

Row 1: Knit to end.

Row 2: Purl to end.

Row 3: K1, m1, knit to last stitch, m1, k1. (9 sts)

Row 4: Purl to end.

Row 5: K1, m1, knit to last stitch, m1, k1. (11 sts)

Row 6: Purl to end.

Work a further 26 rows in St st ending with a WS row.

Next row: K2, sl1, k1, psso, k3, k2tog, k2. (9 sts)

Next row: Purl to end.

Bind off.

Making up

Weave in all loose ends.

Press and block to correct size.

Join front and back body pieces together, leaving top open to insert stuffing.

Join side edges of arms together to create tubes, leaving top open to insert stuffing.

Join legs in the same way as arms.

Join side and top edges of head together, leaving bottom edges open to insert stuffing.

Insert stuffing into body pieces.

Join the top edges of body together.

Join bottom edges of head together.

Stitch the head on to top of body.

Stitch arms into position on the body; place the top of arm at the first shaping marks on body.

Stitch top of legs closed and stitch into position at the bottom of the body.

Embroider faces; add hair and clothes according to the specific patterns for each doll.

Marilyn Monroe

Materials

DOLL

- ★ Wool Cotton by Rowan, approx 122yd/50g ball (50% wool/ 50% cotton)
    - 1 ball in Ecru 900 (MC)
- ★ Scraps of 4-ply cotton in black
- ★ Pair of US 3 (3.25mm) and US 7 (4.50mm) needles
- ★ Fiberfill
- ★ Black embroidery thread
- ★ Scrap of red felt

WHITE DRESS

- ★ Scraps of 4-ply cotton in white (A)
- ★ Old white T-shirt

PINK DRESS

- ★ Aran weight yarn
    - 1 ball in pink (B)
- ★ Scraps of Lurex 4-ply in silver (C)
- ★ Length of wired pink ribbon

Pattern

DOLL

Using MC yarn, make a Basic Doll following the instructions on page 18.

Face

Use leftover black yarn to make eyes. Use red felt to create a mouth, making it slightly wider on one side.

Hair

To create hair, cast on 6 st. Using a looped knitting technique, stitch around the top and back of head.

WHITE DRESS

Bodice

Using US 3 (3.25mm) needles and two strands of yarn A held together, cast on 26 sts.

Work 4 rows in St st.

Next row: Bind off 7 sts, K6, turn. Slip rem stitches on a stitch holder. Working on 6 sts only, work one row of purl.

Next row: Knit to last 3 sts, K2tog, K1. (5 sts)

Next row: Purl.

Next row: Knit to last 3 sts, K2tog, K1. (4 sts)

Next row: Purl.

Work a further 9 rows in St st.

Bind off.

Place sts back on to the needles, with WS facing, bind off 7 sts and purl to end of row.

Work rem sts to match first side, reversing all shapings. Sew back openings together and sew straps together to make a halter neck.

DOB: JUNE 1, 1926
Died: AUGUST 5, 1962
Real name: NORMA JEANE MORTENSON
Hometown: LOS ANGELES, CALIFORNIA

Achievements: "LORELEI LEE" IN *GENTLEMEN PREFER BLONDES*; "THE GIRL" IN *THE SEVEN YEAR ITCH*; "SUGAR KANE" IN *SOME LIKE IT HOT*
Verdict: BLOND BOMBSHELL

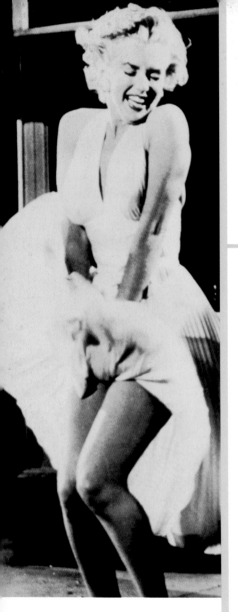

Skirt

Cut a length of fabric from the bottom edge of T-shirt fabric approx 4⅞ in (12cm) deep and 22in (55cm) long. Stitch 4⅞ in (12cm) edges together to form a tube.

Thread a sewing needle and work a running stitch all around the top edge approx ⅛ in (0.5cm) from edge. Repeat this with a second round of running stitch approx ⅜ in (1cm) below the first.

Take the ends of thread and pull to create pleat effect.

Place skirt on doll, and when a snug fit is achieved, tie the threads together. Pin bodice onto skirt and stitch into position.

PINK DRESS

Using US 7 (4.50mm) needles and yarn B, cast on 14 sts.

Row 1: Knit to end.

Row 2: K4, p10.

Rep Rows 1–2 17 times.

Bind off.

With RS facing pick up and knit approx 36 sts along St st edge of bodice.

Row 1: Purl to end.

Row 2: K1, *inc 1, k1, rep from * to end of row.

Work in St st until work measures approx 4⅞ in (12cm) long, ending with a RS row.

Work 2 rows in knit.

Bind off.

Sew side seams together.

First Glove

Using US 3 (3.25mm) needles and yarn B, cast on 7 sts.

Row 1: Purl to end.

Row 2: K1, inc 1, knit to last stitch, inc 1, K1.

Repeat rows 1–2 until 11 sts on needle.

Work 6 rows in St st.

Place bracelet as folls:

Join in yarn C, holding two strands of yarn together.

Next row: K1,*make bobble, k1, rep from * to end.

Break off C.

Knit a further 14 rows in St st.

Bind off.

> ## "The body is meant to be seen, not all covered up."

Second Glove

Using US 3 (3.25mm) needles and yarn B, cast on 7 sts.

Row 1: Purl to end.

Row 2: K1, inc 1, knit to last stitch, inc 1, k1.

Rep Rows 1–2 until 11 sts on needle. Join in yarn C, holding both strands together, knit 5 sts; make bobble in yarn C, knit 6 sts.

Work 20 rows in St st.

Bind off.

Earrings *(make 2)*

Using 4 ends of yarn C together, cast on 2 sts.

Row 1: K1, make bobble.

Bind off.

Materials

DOLL

★ Wool Cotton by Rowan, approx
122yd/50g ball (50% wool/
50% cotton)
    1 ball in Antique 900 (MC)

★ 4-ply Soft by Rowan, approx 191yd/
50g ball (100% wool)
    1 ball in Espresso 389 (A)

★ KidSilk Haze by Rowan, approx
229yd/25g ball (70% kid mohair/
30% silk)
    1 ball in Nightly 585 (B)

★ Pair of US 6 (4.00mm) needles

JUMPSUIT OUTFIT

★ Two pieces of black felt
4 x ¼ in (10 x 0.5cm)
★ Two pieces of black felt
3 x ¼ in (7.5 x 0.5cm)
★ One piece of yellow felt
8 ¾ x 8 ¾ in (22 x 22cm)
★ Sewing thread
★ One snap fastener

PANTS OUTFIT

★ Cotton Glace by Rowan,
approx 137yd/50g ball
(100% cotton)
    1 ball in Black 727 (C)
★ Pair of US 3 (3.25mm) needles
★ One sewing needle

Bruce Lee

Pattern

DOLL

Using MC yarn, make a Basic Doll
following the instructions on page 18.

Face

Using yarn A, embroider face using
picture as guide.

Hair

Using US 6 (4.00mm) needles and yarns
A and B together, cast on 12 sts.

Rows 1–3: Knit.
Row 4: K8, turn.
Row 5: Knit.
Row 6: K4, turn.
Row 7: Knit.
Row 8: K8, turn.
Rows 9–13: Knit.
Row 14: K1, k2tog, knit to end. (11 sts)
Row 15: Knit to last 3 sts, k2tog, k1.
(10 sts)

Row 16: Bind off 4 sts. (6 sts)
Rows 17–22: Knit.
Row 23: K6, cast on 4 sts at end of row.
(10 sts)
Row 24: Knit.
Row 25: Knit to last st, m1, k1. (11 sts)
Row 26: K1, m1, knit to end.
Rows 27–29: Knit.
Row 30: K8, turn.
Row 31: Knit.
Row 32: K4, turn.
Row 33: Knit.
Row 34: K8, turn.
Rows 35–37: Knit.
Bind off.

DOB: NOVEMBER 27, 1940 **Died:** JULY 20, 1973
Nickname: LITTLE DRAGON
Hometown: SAN FRANCISCO, CALIFORNIA
Achievements: "CHEN ZHEN" IN *FIST OF FURY*;
"TANG LONG" IN *WAY OF THE DRAGON*; "LEE" IN *ENTER THE DRAGON*;
"BILLY LO" IN *GAME OF DEATH*; FOUNDER OF JEET KUNE DO
Verdict: MARTIAL ART ICON

Finishing

Sew cast-on and bound-off edges together.

With seam at center, sew top tog. Sew hair onto head with longest side at base of neck and fringe side at top of forehead.

JUMPSUIT

Using templates, cut two of G1, E9, and E6 on pages 103–104.

Use the thin strips of black felt to trim arms and sides, using picture as a guide.

Pin and sew shoulders tog. Pin sleeves into position, making sure center point of sleeve matches shoulder seam and sew tog. Pin and sew sides tog. Pin and sew sleeves tog. Pin and sew inside legs tog. Turn RS out.

Pin and stitch opening cover strip to right-hand side of opening. Using backstitch, sew collar on to jumpsuit. Sew snap fastener to back of collar. Cut black strip to required length for sleeve center to collar and bottom of leg to under arm.

Pin and stitch into position.

PANTS

Legs (make 2)

Using US 3 (3.25mm) needles and yarn C, cast on 19 sts.

Row 1: K1, *p1, k1; rep from * to end.

Row 2: P1, *k1, p1; rep from * to end. These two rows form rib patt. Work a further 4 rows in rib.

Row 7: K2, m1,*k2, m1; rep from * to last st, k1. (28 sts)

Row 8: Purl.

Row 9: Knit.

Work in St st for a further 7 rows, ending with a WS row.

Bind off 2 sts at beg of next 2 rows. (24 sts)

Continue working in St st until work measures approx 4¼ in (11cm) from cast-on edge. Continue in garter stitch for a further ⅜ in (1cm).

Bind off.

"I'm going to be the biggest Chinese Star in the world."

Materials

DOLL

★ Wool Cotton by Rowan, approx
122yd/50g ball (50% wool/
50% cotton)
    1 ball in Antique 900 (MC)
★ 4-ply Soft by Rowan, approx
191yd/50g ball (100% merino wool)
    1 ball in Black 383 (A)
★ KidSilk Haze by Rowan, approx
229yd/25g ball (70% kid mohair/
30% silk)
    1 ball in Nightly 585 (B)
★ Pair of US 6 (4.00mm) needles
★ Fiberfill
★ Black embroidery thread
★ Sewing needle

OUTFIT

★ Three squares of white felt
8¾ x 8¾ in (22 x 22cm)
★ Three squares of black felt
8¾ x 8¾ in (22 x 22cm)
★ One press stud
★ Six small black buttons
★ Black sewing thread

"I walk slowly, but I will never walk backward."

Abraham Lincoln

Pattern

DOLL

Using MC yarn, make a Basic Doll following the instructions on page 18.

Face

Using yarn A, embroider face using picture as guide.

Hair

Using yarns A and B together and US6 (4mm) needles, cast on 10 sts.

Row 1: Knit to end.
Row 2: Knit to end.
Row 3: K2, inc 1, knit to last 2 sts, m1, k2. (12 sts)
Row 4: Knit.
Rep Rows 2 and 3 until 18 sts.
Row 11: Knit to end.
Row 12: Purl to end.

Rows 13–14: Cast off 3 sts at beg of next two rows. (12 sts)
Row 15: K1, ssk, knit to last 3 sts, k2tog, k1. (10 sts)
Row 16: Purl to end.
Rep Rows 15 and 16 until 4 sts.
Work a further 3 rows keeping St st sequence correct.
Bind off.
Turn back 4 sts onto main fabric and stitch slightly to the left to create small quiff.

Beard

Using yarns A and B together and US 6 (4mm) needles, cast on 3 sts.

Rows 1–6: Knit.
Row 7: K2, m1, k1. (4 sts)
Work 6 rows Knit.
Row 14: K1, k2tog, k2. (3 sts)
Work 6 rows knit.
Bind off.
Place hair on basic doll head, stitch into position. Pin beard to face and stitch into position.

OUTFIT

Double-breasted Jacket

Using templates, cut out front (2 x F2), back (K1), sleeves (2 x E9), and collar (F1) from black felt.
Sew as close to the edge as possible.
Pin and sew shoulders together.
Pin sleeves into position, making sure center point of sleeve matches shoulder seam and sew together. Pin and sew sides together. Pin and sew sleeves together. Turn RS out.
Fold collar in half and pin together; stitch as close to edge as possible to create fold. Pin and stitch collar into position. Sew press stud to inside of jacket and stitch 6 buttons into position on front, using picture as guide.

Pants

Using template, cut out front and back of trousers (2 x E8). Pin WS together and stitch sides. Turn RS out.

Shirt

Make as for The Beatles Mop Top Shirt on page 72.

DOB: FEBRUARY 12, 1809
Death: APRIL 15, 1865
Hometown: HARDIN COUNTY, KENTUCKY

Achievements: 16TH PRESIDENT OF THE UNITED STATES, 1861–1865; ABOLISHED SLAVERY
Verdict: ICONIC EMANCIPATOR

Jackie O

Materials

DOLL

- ★ Wool Cotton by Rowan, approx 122yd/50g ball (50% wool/ 50% cotton)
  - 1 ball in Ecru 900 (MC)
- ★ 4-ply Soft by Rowan, approx 191yd/50g ball (100% merino wool)
  - 1 ball in Espresso 389 (A)
- ★ KidSilk Haze by Rowan, approx 229yd/25g ball (70% kid mohair/ 30% silk)
  - 1 ball in Villain 584 (B)
- ★ Pair of US 3 (3.25mm) needles
- ★ Black embroidery thread
- ★ Small piece of pink felt for mouth

COAT DRESS

- ★ Two squares pale blue nylon felt 8¾ x 8¾in (22 x 22cm)
- ★ Matching sewing cotton
- ★ Three snap fasteners

LITTLE BLACK DRESS

- ★ Square black nylon felt 8¾ x 8¾in (22 x 22cm)
- ★ Black and white sewing thread
- ★ Piece white nylon felt 6 x 3in (15 x 7.5cm)
- ★ Cotton Glace by Rowan, approx 137yd/50g ball (100% cotton)
  - 1 ball in Bleached 726 (B)

Pattern

DOLL

Using MC yarn, make a Basic Doll following the instructions on page 18.

Face

Using picture as guide, embroider face and create a mouth using pink felt.

Hair

Using yarn A and B tog and US 3 (3.25mm) needles, cast on 14 sts.

Row 1: Knit.
Row 2: Purl.
Row 3: K2, m1, knit to last 2 sts, m1, k2. (16 sts)
Row 4: Purl.
Rep Rows 3 and 4 until 22 sts.
Next row: Cast on 18 sts and knit to end. (40 sts)
Next row: Purl.
Next row: *K2, k2tog; rep from * to end. (30 sts)
Next row: Purl.
Next row: *K1, k2tog; rep from * to end (20 sts)
Next row: [P2tog] rep to end. (10 sts)
Break off yarn, leaving approx 6in (15cm), thread through sts on needle and pull tight, secure yarn and sew side together.

With front RS facing, pick up and knit 22 sts from side seam to cast-on edge; you will be picking up with the purl side facing.

Right Hand Flick

Row 1: Purl.
Row 2: K2, ssk, knit to end (21 sts)
Row 3: P1, p2tog, p12, turn.
Row 4: K11, ssk, k1.
Row 5: P10, turn.
Row 6: K7, ssk, k1.
Row 7: P8, turn.
Row 8: K5, ssk, k1.

DOB: JULY 28, 1929
Died: MAY 19, 1994
Real name: JACQUELINE LEE BOUVIER
Hometown: SOUTHAMPTON, NEW YORK

Achievements: FIRST LADY OF THE UNITED STATES, 1961–1963; IMPECCABLE DRESS SENSE
Verdict: STYLE ICON

Bind off.

Turn back onto main part of hair and stitch ¾ in (2cm) along from side seam to cast-on edge.

Left Hand Flick

With front RS facing, pick up and knit 10 sts from cast-on edge to seam; you will be picking up with the purl side facing.

Row 1: Purl.

Row 2: K8, turn.

Row 3: Purl to last 3 sts, p2tog, p1.

Row 4: K6, turn.

Row 5: Purl.

Row 6: K4, turn.

Row 7: Purl.

Row 8: Knit.

Bind off.

Fold over and stitch into place.

COAT DRESS

Using templates, cut out right and left front (2 x E3), back (K1), sleeves (2 x E9), and collar (E6).

Cut out 2 strips to match the front length of coat and approx ¾ in (2cm) wide for front placket. Sew all edges as close to the edge as possible.

Cut out 2 small rounded bottom pockets to fit on front.

Pin and sew shoulders together.

Pin sleeves into position, making sure center point of sleeve matches shoulder seam and sew together.

Pin and sew sides tog; pin and sew sleeves tog. Turn RS out.

With RS together, pin front placket to coat front opening and stitch into position. Press with a cool iron and damp cloth so as not to damage the fabric. Pin and stitch collar into position. Pin and stitch pockets to front, using picture as a guide for positioning.

Sew three small snap fasteners to front opening of jacket, at the top, middle, and bottom.

"The first time you marry for love, the second for money, and the third for companionship."

LITTLE BLACK DRESS

Dress

Using template, cut out front and back from black felt (2 x L2).

Sew as close to the edge as possible. Pin and sew shoulders together. Pin and sew sides together. Turn RS out.

Pill Box Hat

Using template, cut out hat top (L3) and side (L4).

Using backstitch, sew side along edge of hat top. Sew tog along side seam.

White Gloves

Using US 3 (3.25mm) needles and yarn B, cast on 8 sts.

Row 1: Knit.

Row 2: Purl.

Row 3: K1, m1, knit to last sts, m1, k1. (10 sts)

Row 4: Purl.

Row 5: As Row 3. (12 sts)

Row 6: Purl.

Work in St st for a further 6 rows or required length. Bind off.

Beads

Thread approx 50 small white beads onto a strong thread, tie ends together.

Sunglasses

Using US 3 (3.25mm) needles and yarn, cast on 2sts.

Row 1: Knit.

Row 2: Knit.

Repeat rows 1–2 once more.

Row 5: K1, inc 1, K1. (3 sts)

Row 6: Purl.

Row 7: K2, inc1, k1. (4 sts)

Row 8: Purl.

Row 9: K2, k2tog. (3 sts)

Row 10: Purl.

Row 11: K1, k2tog. (2 sts)

Repeat from row 5–11 once more.

Knit 4 rows. Bind off.

Che Guevara

Materials

DOLL

★ Wool Cotton by Rowan, approx 122yd/50g ball (50% wool/ 50% cotton)

    1 ball in Antique 900 (MC)

★ Kid Classic by Rowan, approx 153 yd/50g ball (70% lambswool, 26% kid mohair, 4% nylon)

    1 ball in Black 007 (A)

★ 4-ply Soft by Rowan, approx 192yd/50g ball (100% wool)

    1 ball in Black 383 (B)

OUTFIT

★ Square of khaki cotton (or old pair of army pants) 8¾ x 8¾ in (22 x 22cm)

★ Square khaki green jersey stretch fabric (or old T-shirt) 8¾ x 8¾ in (22 x 22cm)

Pattern

DOLL

Using MC yarn, make a Basic Doll following the instructions on page 18.

Face

Using black 4-ply soft yarn, embroider face, using picture as guide.

Eyes: French knots.

Eyebrows: Backstitch.

Sideburns: Work 2 long backstitches at either side of face in yarn A.

Mustache: Work a long backstitch at top of mouth and long backstitch down toward chin.

Hair

Using US 6 (4.00mm) needle and yarn A, cast on 10 sts.

Row 1: Knit.

Row 2: Purl.

Row 3: K2, m1, knit to last 2 sts, M1, k2. (12 sts)

Row 4: Purl. Rep Rows 3 and 4 until 18 sts.

Row 11: Knit.

Row 12: Purl.

Rows 13–14: Bind off 3 sts at beg of next 2 rows. (12 sts)

Keep working in St st and bind off 2 sts at beg of each row until 4 sts.

Bind off 4 sts.

Sew in all loose ends, pin, and stitch into position on head.

Using yarn A, cut approx 30 lengths 6in (15cm) long.

Taking 2–3 strands at a time, fold in half and, using a crochet hook, pull through front edge of hair and loop back on itself like a tassel. Cut to required length using picture as guide.

OUTFIT

Pants

Using template, cut out front and back of trousers (2 x E8). Pin WS together and stitch sides. Turn RS out.

T-shirt

Using template, cut out front (H7), back (H6), and sleeves (2 x H5). Place RS of fabric together, pin and stitch side seams and arms together, and sew. Stitch top of arms from neck to cuff and stitch side seams together; turn RS out. Press seams with steam iron.

DOB: JUNE 14, 1928
Died: OCTOBER 9, 1967
Real name: ERNESTO GUEVARA DE LA SERNA
Hometown: ROSARIO, ARGENTINA

Achievements: MARXIST REVOLUTIONARY, MEDIC, POLITICAL FIGURE, AND LEADER OF CUBAN AND INTERNATIONALIST GUERRILLAS
Verdict: REVOLUTIONARY ICON

Jimi Hendrix

Materials

DOLL

★ Wool Cotton by Rowan, approx 122yd/50g ball (50% wool/ 50% cotton)
   1 ball in Mocha 965(MC)
★ Kid Classic by Rowan, approx 151 yd/50g ball (70% lambswool, 30% kid mohair, 4% nylon)
   1 ball in Black (A)
★ 4-ply Soft by Rowan, approx 191 yd/50 g ball (100% pure new wool)
   1 ball in Black 383 (B)
★ Pair of US 3 (3.25mm) needles

OUTFIT

★ Psychedelic-print cotton fabric 10 x 10in (25 x 25cm)
★ Mediumweight khaki cotton or old pair of army pants 10 x 10in (25 x 25cm)
★ Pink felt fabric 8¾ x 8¾ in (22 x 22cm)
★ Two small snap fasteners
★ Pink, green, and white sewing thread

Pattern

DOLL

Using MC yarn, make a Basic Doll following the instructions on page 18.

Face

Embroider face onto head, using black yarn/embroidery thread.
If using 4-ply Soft, split yarn down and use two strands tog for eyes and one strand for mouth.
Eyes: French knot with thread 4–5 times round needle.
Mouth: Backstitch.

Hair

Special abbreviation:
L1 = loop 1: Insert knitwise needle into next st, bring first 2 fingers on left hand under RH needle, take yarn over needle and under finger twice, take yarn over and under needle, do not take finger out of loops, pull all 3 loops on RH needle back through st on LH needle and slip LH st off needle, slip 3 loops back onto LH needle and knit as normal. It is important to keep finger in the loops until knitted.
Using US 6 (4.00mm) needle and yarns A and B tog, cast on 11 sts.

Row 1: Knit.
Row 2: K1, *L1, k1; rep from * to end.
Row 3: K1, m1, k to last st, m1, k1.
(13 sts)
Rep last 2 rows until 19 sts.
Row 9: Knit.
Row 10: K2,*L1, k1; rep from * to last st, k1.
Row 11: Knit.

★ ★ ★

DOB: NOVEMBER 27, 1942
Died: SEPTEMBER 18, 1970
Hometown: SEATTLE, WASHINGTON
Achievements: ONE OF THE GREATEST AND MOST INFLUENTIAL GUITARISTS IN ROCK MUSIC HISTORY. HE HAD HITS SUCH AS, "HEY JOE," "STONE FREE," AND "PURPLE HAZE."
Verdict: GUITAR LEGEND ICON

Row 12: K1, *L1, k1; rep from * to end.
Row 13: Bind off 3 sts at beg of row, knit to end. (16 sts)
Row 14: Bind off 3 sts, k1, *L1, k1; rep from * to end. (13 sts)
Row 15: K1, ssk, knit to last 3 sts, k2tog, k1. (11 sts)
Row 16: K1, *L1, k1; rep from * to end. Rep Rows 15–16 until you have 9 sts.
Next row: Knit.
Next row: K2, *L1, k1; rep from * to last st, k1.
Bind off.
Sew in all loose ends, pin hair to head, and stitch into position.

OUTFIT

Shirt

Using templates and printed cotton, cut out front and back of shirt (2 x M3), collars (2 x M2), sleeve tops (2 x Q2) and bottoms (Q1), button bands (2 x M4), 2 cuffs (P2).
Leave ¼ in (0.5cm) seam throughout.

Button Bands (make 2)

Using steam iron, fold up and press approx ⅜ in (1cm) in toward the center, then fold down rest of fabric.
With folded edges to the RS, place shirt edge into folds of button band; pin and stitch into position. Trim excess fabric.
Place RS of shirt back and front tog and pin and stitch shoulders.

Sleeves (make 2)

Work 2 rows of running stitch along top and bottom of sleeve bottom, pull tight to form a ruffle; make sure fabric is same width as sleeve top. Turn up ¼ in (0.5cm) hem at bottom of sleeve top, pin and stitch to top of ruffle, and stitch into position.

Cuffs (make 2)

Using steam iron, fold up and press approx ⅜ in (1cm) in toward the center, then fold down rest of fabric.
With folded edges to the RS, place ruffle into cuff, pin and stitch into position.
Fold sleeves in half, mark halfway point, match up to shoulder seam. With right sides facing, pin and stitch.
Pin and stitch sleeve and side seams tog. Turn RS out and press all seams.

Collar

With RS tog, stitch along the sides and curved edge; leave straight edge open. Turn RS out, and use knitting needle or similar blunt point to poke out collar.

Press using steam iron to flatten seams. Pin and stitch to shirt.
Sew snap fastener onto button band.

Pants

Using template and green fabric, cut out front and back of pants (2 x D1).
With RS tog, pin and stitch outer and inner side seams together.
Turn RS out and press fabric with steam iron. Fold in approx ⅜ in (1cm) hem at waist, and stitch. Fold in approx ⅜ in (1cm) hem at legs, and stitch.

Vest

Using template and pink fabric, cut out vest back (Q3) and front (2 x Q4).
Sew shoulders tog. Sew side seams together, leaving approx 1¾ in (4cm) opening at top for armhole.
Turn RS out and press.

Headband

Cut a 2in (5cm) strip of fabric; using steam iron, fold up and press approx ¾ in (2cm) in toward the center, then fold down rest of fabric. Stitch down the center to secure.

Albert Einstein

Materials

DOLL

★ Wool Cotton by Rowan, approx
  122yd/50g ball (50% wool/
  50% cotton)
    1 ball in Ecru 900 (MC)
    1 ball in Ship Shape 955 (C)
★ KidSilk Haze by Rowan, approx
  229 yd/25g ball, (70% kid mohair,
  30% silk)
    1 ball in Pearl 590 (A)
★ Scottish Tweed by Rowan,
  approx 131 yd/25g ball
  (100% wool)
    1 ball in Gray Mist 001 (B)

★ 4-ply Soft by Rowan, approx 191yd/
  50g ball (100% wool)
    1 ball in Black 383 (D)
★ Pair US 3 (3.25mm) and US 6
  (4.00mm) needles
★ Black felt
  8¾ x 8¾ in (22 x 22cm)
★ Matching thread

DOB: MARCH 14, 1879
Died: APRIL 18, 1955
Nickname: TETE
Home town: ULM,
WURTTEMBERG, GERMANY

Achievements: $E = mc^2$;
NOBEL PRIZE IN PHYSICS, 1921
Verdict: THE BRAINY ICON

Pattern

DOLL

Using MC yarn, make a Basic Doll
following the instructions on page 18.

Face

Using D, embroider the face.
Eyes: French knots.
Eyebrows: Backstitch.

Mustache

Using yarns A and B tog, cast on 6 sts.
Work 2 rows in garter st, bind off.
Pin and stitch onto face.

Hair

Using yarn A and B tog throughout and
US 3 (3.25mm) needles, cast on 12 sts.
Rows 1–3: Knit.
Row 4: K8, turn.
Row 5: Knit to end.
Row 6: K4, turn.
Row 7: Knit to end.
Row 8: K8, turn.
Rows 9–13: Knit to end.
Row 14: K1, k2tog, knit to end. (11 sts)
Row 15: Knit to last 3 sts, k2tog, k1.
(10 sts)
Row 16: Bind off 4 sts. (6 sts)
Rows 17–19: Knit.
Row 20: Bind off 2 sts at beg of row,
knit to end. (4 sts)
Row 21: K4, cast on 2 sts.
Row 22: Knit to end.

Row 23: K6, cast on 4 sts at end of row. (10 sts)

Row 24: Knit to end.

Row 25: Knit to last st, m1, k1. (11 sts)

Row 26: K1, m1, knit to end.

Rows 27–29: Knit to end.

Row 30: K8, turn.

Row 31: Knit to end.

Row 32: K4, turn.

Row 33: Knit to end.

Row 34: K8, turn.

Rows 35–37: Knit to end.

Bind off.

Sew cast-on and bound-off edges tog. With seam at center, sew top tog. Place on head and stitch into position. Using yarns A and B tog, cut approx 30 lengths 6in (15cm) long. Taking 2–3 strands at a time, fold in half and using a crochet hook pull through front edge of hair and loop back on itself like a tassel. Cut to required length using picture as guide.

OUTFIT

Sweater

Back

Using yarn C and US 3 (3.25mm) needles, cast on 19 sts.

Row 1: K1, *p1, k1, rep from * to end.
Row 2: P1, *K1, p1, rep from * to end.
Rep Rows 1 and 2 once more.
Change to US 6 (4.00mm) needles.
Row 5: Knit to end.
Row 6: Purl to end.
Rep Rows 5-6 four more times.

Shape armholes

Bind off 2 sts at the beg of the next two rows. (15 sts)
Work 8 rows in St st.

Front

Using yarn C and US 3 (3.25mm) needles, cast on 19 sts.

Row 1: K1, *p1, k1, rep from * to end.
Row 2: P1, *K1, p1, rep from * to end.
Repeat rows 1–2 once more.
Change to US 6 (4.00mm) needles.
Row 5: Knit to end.
Row 6: Purl to end.
Rep Rows 5 and 6 four more times.

Shape armholes

Bind off 2 sts at the beg of the next two rows. (15 sts)
Work 2 rows in St st.

Shape neck

Row 1: K6, turn (leave rem sts on needle or transfer to stitch holder).
Row 2: P1, p2tog, purl to end. (5 sts)
Row 3: K4, k2tog, k1. (4 sts)
Work 3 rows in St st.
Bind off.
Rejoin yarn to sts, bind off 3 sts, knit to end. (6 sts)
Next row: Purl to last 3 sts, p2tog tbl, p1. (5 sts)
Next row: K1, sl2, k1, psso, k3. (4 sts)
Work 3 rows in St st.
Bind off.

Sleeves (make 2)

Using yarn C and US 3 (3.25mm) needles, cast on 15 sts.
Row 1: K1, *p1, k1, rep from * to end.
Row 2: P1, *K1, p1, rep from * to end.
Repeat rows 1–2 once more.
Change to US 6 (4.00mm) needles.
Row 5: Knit to end.
Row 6: Purl to end.
Rep Rows 5–6 ten more times.
Bind off.

Finishing

Sew in all loose ends, sew RH shoulder tog, and work neckband as follows.

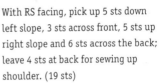

With RS facing, pick up 5 sts down left slope, 3 sts across front, 5 sts up right slope and 6 sts across the back; leave 4 sts at back for sewing up shoulder. (19 sts)
Row 1: P1, *K1, p1; rep from * to end.
Row 2: K1, *p1, k1; rep from * to end.
Bind off in rib using US 6 (4.00mm) needle.

Pants

Using template, cut out front and back (2 x E8) from black felt. Leave ¼ in (0.5cm) seam throughout.
Pin WS together and stitch sides. Turn RS out.

Cher

Materials

DOLL

- ★ Wool Cotton by Rowan, approx 122yd/50g ball (50% wool/ 50% cotton)
  - 1 ball in Ecru 900 (MC)
- ★ Kid Classic by Rowan, approx 153y/50g ball (70% lambswool, 26% kid mohair, 4% nylon)
  - 1 ball in Smoke 831 (A)
- ★ 4-ply Soft by Rowan, approx 191 yd/50g ball (100% merino wool)
  - 1 ball in Expresso 389 (B)
- ★ Pair US 6 (4.00mm) needles
- ★ Small piece red felt fabric for lips

TURN BACK TIME

- ★ KidSilk Haze by Rowan, approx 229 yd/25g ball (70% kid mohair, 30% silk)
  - 1 ball in Nightly 585 (C)
- ★ Black felt 8¾ x 8¾ in (22 x 22cm)
- ★ Black fake leather or vinyl 10 x 10in (25 x 25cm)
- ★ Black and white sewing cotton
- ★ Two small snap fasteners
- ★ Tube silver sequins

SHIFT DRESS

- ★ Pink felt 22 x 22cm (8¾ x 8¾ in)
- ★ Printed cotton fabric 22 x 22cm (8¾ x 8¾ in)
- ★ Gluestick

Pattern

DOLL

Using MC yarn, make a Basic Doll following the instructions on page 18.

Face

Cut out lip shape from red felt and stitch onto face.

Embroider face onto head, using embroidery thread.

If using 4-ply Soft, split yarn down and use two strands together for eyes and one strand for mouth.

Eyes: French knot, wrapping thread around needle approx 4–5 times.

TURN BACK TIME

Hair

Special abbreviation:

L1 = loop 1: Insert knitwise needle into next st, bring first 2 fingers on left hand under RH needle, take yarn over the needle and under finger twice, take yarn over and under needle, do not take finger out of loops; pull all 3 loops on RH needle back through st on LH needle and slip LH st off needle, slip 3 loops back onto LH needle, and knit as normal. It is important to keep finger in the loops until knitted.

DOB: MAY 20, 1946
Real Name: CHERYL SARKISIAN LAPIERE
Hometown: EL CENTRO, CALIFORNIA
Achievements: AN OSCAR, A GRAMMY, AN EMMY, AND THREE GOLDEN GLOBE AWARDS FOR HER ACCOMPLISHMENTS ACROSS MUSIC, FILM, AND TELEVISION. CHER HAS HAD NUMBER ONE HITS AS A SOLO ARTIST WITH "BELIEVE" (1999) AND ALSO "I GOT YOU BABE" (1965) AS PART OF THE "SONNY AND CHER" DUO.
Verdict: AGELESS ICON

Using US 6 (4.00mm) needle and yarn A, cast on 15 sts.

Row 1: Knit.

Row 2: K1, *L1, k1; rep from * to end.

Row 3: K1, m1, knit to last st, m1, k1. (17 sts)

Rep last 2 rows once more. (19 sts)

Row 6: Knit to end.

Row 7: K2,* L1, k1; rep from * to last st, k1.

Row 8: Knit.

Row 9: K1, *L1, k1; rep from * to end.

Rep Rows 6–9 once more.

Row 13: K1, k2tog, knit to last 3 sts, k2tog, k1.

Row 14: K1, *L1, k1; rep from * to end.

Rep last two rows until 11 sts.

Bind off purlwise.

Sew in all loose ends, pin hair to head, and stitch into position.

Tights *(make 2)*

Using yarn C and US 6 (4.00mm) needles, cast on 14 sts.

Row 1: Knit.

Row 2: K1, *yfwd, sl1, k1, psso, k1; rep from * to end.

Rep last row 7 times.

Row 9: K3tog, *yfwd, ssk, m; rep from * to last 5 sts, yfwd, ssk, k3tog. (10 sts)

Place marker at beg and end of row.

Work a further 22 rows as Row 2.

Next row: Knit to end.

Next row: K5, fold knitting in half; with both needles in left hand, take a 3rd needle and bind off both needles together.

Break off yarn, leaving 8in (20cm) length to sew up side of tights until dec row markers.

Sew right and left leg to together.

Bodysuit

Using template and black felt, cut out the suit (J1).

Stitch tights to outfit.

Sew snap fasteners to straps.

Jacket

Using templates and fake leather, cut out front (2 x E2), back (E1), and sleeves (2 x E9).

Sew shoulders tog. Fold sleeves in half, mark halfway point, match up to shoulder seam. With RS facing, pin and stitch. Cut front center open to create jacket opening. Pin and stitch sleeve and side seams tog.

Turn RS out and press all seams.

Turn approx ½in (1.5cm) of fabric at front inside and pin and stitch.

SHIFT DRESS

Hair

Using US 3 (3.25mm) needles and yarn A, cast on 10 sts.

Row 1: Knit.

Row 2: Purl.

Row 3: K2, m1, knit to last 2 sts, m1, k2. (12 sts)

Row 4: Purl.

Rep Rows 2 and 3 until 18 sts.

Rows 11–14: Work in St st.

Keep working in St st every row.

Bind off 2 sts at beg of next two rows. (14 sts)

Bind off 1 st at beg of next two rows. (12 sts)

Bind off 2 sts at beg of next two rows. (8 sts)

Bind off.

Cut 30 lengths of yarn A approx 12in (30cm) long.

Taking 2–3 strands at a time, fold in half and using a crochet hook, pull through front edge of hair and loop back on itself like a tassel; use picture as guide.

Dress

Using template, cut out front and back (2 x L2) from pink felt. Pin and sew shoulders together, leave opening of approx 2in (5cm) for armhole, and sew up side seams. Turn dress right side out.

Cut out circular motifs from fabric, and using suitable fabric glue, stick to front of dress, using photo as guideline for positioning.

"Men aren't necessities. They're luxuries."

James Dean

Materials

DOLL

★ Wool Cotton by Rowan, approx
122yd/50g ball (50% wool/
50% cotton)
1 ball in Ecru 900 (MC)
★ Cotton Glace by Rowan, approx
124yd/50g ball (100% cotton)
1 ball in Bleached 726 (A)
★ Tapestry by Rowan, approx
131yd/50g ball (70% wool/
30% soya bean)
1 ball in Antique 173 (B)
★ KidSilk Haze by Rowan, approx
229yd/25g ball (70% kid mohair/
30% silk)
1 ball in Pearl 590 (C)
★ Pair of US 3 (3.25mm) needles
★ Pair of US 6 (4.00mm) needles

OUTFIT

★ Red felt
8¾ x 8¾ in (22 x 22cm)
★ Denim fabric
8¾ x 8¾ in (22 x 22cm)
★ 1 x 3¼ in (8cm) red zipper

Pattern

DOLL

Using MC yarn, make a Basic Doll following the instructions on page 18.

Face

Using yarn A, embroider face using picture as guide.

Hair

Using yarns B and C tog and US 6 (4.00mm) needles, cast on 10 sts.
Note: As the tapestry yarn is variegated, start knitting with the lighter shaded area.
Row 1: Knit.
Row 2: Purl.
Row 3: K2, m1, knit to last 2 sts, m1, k2. (12 sts)
Row 4: Purl.
Rep Rows 2 and 3 until 18 sts.
Rows 11–14: Work in St st.
Keep working in St st for every row.

Bind off 2 sts at beg of next two rows. (14 sts)
Bind off 1 st at beg of next two rows. (12 sts)
Bind off 2 sts at beg of next two rows. (8 sts)
Bind off.
With bound-off edge facing, pick up and knit 10 sts across front; you will be working with the purl side facing.
Row 1: Purl.
Row 2: K2, ssk, knit to 4 sts, k2tog, k2. (8 sts)
Rep Rows 1 and 2 once more. (6 sts)
Row 5: K1, sl1, k2tog, psso, k2. (4 sts)
Row 6: Purl.
Row 7: Knit.
Bind off.

★ ★ ★

DOB: FEBRUARY 8, 1931
Died: SEPTEMBER 30, 1955
Real name: JAMES BYRON DEAN
Nickname: JIMMY DEAN
Hometown: MARION, INDIANA

Achievements:
"JIM STARK" IN *REBEL WITHOUT A CAUSE*; "JETT RINK" IN *GIANT*
Verdict: REBELLIOUS ICON

Turn back 4 sts onto main fabric and stitch slightly to the left to create quiff. Place hair on basic doll head and stitch into position.

Using black 4-ply soft, embroider face using picture as guide.

OUTFIT

Jacket

Using templates and red felt, cut out right and left front (2 x E2), back (E1), sleeves (2 x E9), and collar (E6) from red felt. Leave ¼ in (0.5cm) seam throughout.

Pin and sew shoulders tog. Pin sleeves into position, making sure center point of sleeve matches shoulder seam and sew tog. Pin and sew sides tog. Pin and sew sleeves tog, leaving approx ½ in (1.5cm) at cuff opening.

Turn RS out. Pin and stitch collar into position. Stitch zip to front of jacket.

Sweater

Using yarn A throughout, work as given for Elvis's T-shirt on page 99.

Jeans

Using template and denim fabric, cut out front and back of trousers (2 x E8). Pin WS together and stitch sides. Turn RS out.

Muhammad Ali

Materials

DOLL

★ Wool Cotton by Rowan, approx
  122yd/50g ball (50% wool/
  50% cotton)
      1 ball in Coffee Rich 956 (MC)
★ Cotton Glace by Rowan, approx
  124yd/50g ball (100% cotton)
      1 ball in Bleached 726 (A)
      1 ball in Blood Orange 445 (B)
★ Pair of US3 (3.25mm) and US 6
  (4.00mm) needles

OUTFIT

★ KidSilk Haze by Rowan, approx
  229yd/25g ball (70% kid mohair/
  30% silk)
      1 ball in Nightly 585 (C)
★ 4-ply Soft by Rowan, approx
  191yd/50g ball (100% merino wool)
      1 ball in Black 383 (D)
★ Two thin strips of black felt
★ Sewing needle/embroidery needle

Pattern

DOLL

Using MC yarn, make a Basic Doll
following the instructions on page 18.

Face

Using yarn C, embroider face using
picture as guide.

Hair

Using yarns A and B together
throughout and US 6 (4.00mm)
needles, cast on 10 sts and knit in
garter stitch as
follows:
Row 1: Knit.
Row 2: Knit.
Row 3: K2, m1, k
to last 2 sts, inc1,
k2. (12 sts)
Row 4: Knit.
Repeat rows 2 and
3 until 18 sts.
Rows 11–14: Knit.

Keep working in garter stitch for every
row.
Bind off 2 sts at beg of next two rows.
(14 sts)
Bind off 1 st at beg of next two rows.
(12 sts)
Bind off 2 sts at beg of next two rows.
(8 sts)
Bind off 2 sts at beg of next two rows.
(4 sts)
Next row: (K2tog) twice. (2 sts)
Bind off.
Place hair on basic doll with
cast-on edge halfway up back
of head and bound-off edge
at top of forehead, then
stitch into position.

★ ★ ★

DOB: JANUARY 17, 1942
Real name: CASSIUS CLAY, JR.
Nickname: THE GREATEST
Hometown: LOUISVILLE, KENTUCKY

Achievements: THREE-TIME WORLD
HEAVYWEIGHT BOXING CHAMPION; DEFEATED
GEORGE FOREMAN IN "THE RUMBLE IN THE
JUNGLE" (1974)
VERDICT: HEAVYWEIGHT ICON

"I'll be floating like a butterfly and stinging like a bee."

OUTFIT

Boxing Gloves *(make 2)*

Using yarn B and US 3 (3.25mm) needles, cast on 11sts.

Row 1: *P1, k1; rep from * to end.
Row 2: P1, *k1, p1; rep from * to end.

These two rows form rib pattern; work a further 4 rows in rib.

Row 7: Knit.
Row 8: Purl.
Row 9: K1, *m1, k1; rep from * to end. (21 sts)
Row 10: Purl.
Row 11: Knit.

Work a further 3 rows in St st.

Row 15: K1, *k2tog, k1; rep from * to last 2 sts, k2. (15 sts)
Row 16: Purl.

Row 17: K1, *k2tog; rep fom * to last 2 sts, k2. (9 sts)
Row 18: P1, *p2tog; rep from * to end. (5 sts)

Break off yarn, leaving approx 6in (15cm) of yarn.

Thread yarn through sts on needle, pull tight, and secure yarn. Sew tog side seam; secure yarn.

Take small amount of yarn A and thread through ribbed fabric like shoe laces from cast-on edge toward top of glove and tie a bow.

Insert stuffing to bulbous part of glove.

Shorts *(make 2)*

Using yarn A and US 3 (3.25mm) needles, cast on 19 sts.

Row 1: K1, *p1, k1; rep from * to end.
Row 2: P1, *k1, p1; rep from * to end.

These two rows form rib pattern; work a further 4 rows in rib.

Row 7: K2, m1, *k2, m1; rep from * to last st, k1. (28 sts)
Row 8: Purl.
Row 9: Knit.

Work in St st for a further 7 rows, ending with a WS row.

Bind off 2 sts at beg of next 2 rows. (24 sts)

Continue working in St st until work measures approx 3¼ in (8cm) from cast-on edge.

Bind off.

Place two pieces tog, matching side seams, front and back crotch, and inside leg seams. Stitch seams using a backstitch or a mattress stitch close to the edge. Cut two strips of black felt ½ x 3in (1.5 x 8.5cm); pin and stitch to side of shorts.

King Kong

Materials

DOLL

★ Wool Cotton by Rowan, approx
122yd/50g ball (50% wool/
50% cotton)
   1 ball in 382 (MC)
★ Kid Classic by Rowan, approx
142yds/50gm ball (70% lambswool,
26% kid mohair, 4% nylon)
   1 ball in Peat 832 (A)
★ 4-ply Soft by
Rowan, approx
191yd/50g ball
(100% wool)
   1 ball in
   Victoria 390 (B)
★ Small amount of
red, white and black
nylon felt
★ US 6 (4.00mm)
needles

Hometown: SKULL ISLAND, INDIAN OCEAN/JAPAN
Achievements: SCALING THE EMPIRE STATE BUILDING
Verdict: SIMIAN ICON

Pattern

BODY *(make 2)*
Using yarn MC and US 6 (4.00mm)
needles, cast on 14 sts.
Row 1: Knit.
Row 2: Purl.
Row 3: K1, inc 1, knit to last sts, inc 1,
k1. (16 sts)
Row 4: Purl.
Row 5: As Row 3. (18 sts)
Row 6: Purl.
Rows 7–14: Work in St
st, starting with a knit
row.
Row 15: As Row 3.
(20 sts)
Rows 16–18: Work in
St st, ending with a
purl row.
Row 19: K1, sl1, k1,
psso, knit to last 3
sts, k2tog, k1.
(18 sts)
Rows 20–22: Work
in St st, ending
with a purl row.
Row 23: As Row
19. (16 sts)
Row 24: Purl.

Row 25: As row 19. (14 sts)
Row 26: Purl.
Bind off.

HEAD
Front and Back
Using US 6 (4.00mm) needles and yarn
MC, cast on 14 sts.
Row 1: Knit.
Row 2: Purl.
Rep Rows 1 and 2 twice more.
Row 7: K1, sl1, k1, psso, knit to last
3 sts, k2tog, k1. (12 sts)
Rows 8–10: Work in St st.
Row 11: As Row 7. (10 sts)
Rows 12–14: Work in St st.
Row 15: As Row 7. (8 sts)
Rows 16–20: Work in St st.
Change to yarn B.
Rows 21–24: Work in St st.
Change back to yarn A.
Create eyebrow as follows:
Row 25: When working this row, pick up
purl loop 4 rows previously worked and
work tog with stitch on needle.
Rows 26–28: Work in St st.
Row 29: K2, join in A, k4, turn (work on
these 4 sts only).
Next row: P4, turn.
Next row: Knit into front and back of

next 4 sts. (8 sts)

Work 3 rows St st.

Next row: [Sl1, k1, psso] twice, [k2tog] twice. (4 sts)

Next row: Purl.

Using brown yarn, work next 4 sts as Row 25, k2sts to end.

Rows 30–37: Work in St st.

Bind off.

Head Sides (make 2)

Using yarn MC and US 6 (4.00mm) needles cast on 10 sts.

Row 1: Knit.

Row 2: Purl.

Rep last 2 rows twice more.

Row 7: K1, sl1, k1, psso, knit to last 3 sts, k2tog. (8 sts)

Row 8: Purl.

Row 9: Knit.

Row 10: Purl.

Row 11: As row 7.

Row 12: Purl.

Bind off.

Ears (make 2)

Using yarn MC and US 6 (4.00mm) needles, cast on 6 sts.

Work 4 rows in knit. Break off yarn, leaving approx 4in (10cm); thread through sts and pull tight.

Face

Using template and white felt, cut out two sets of spikes for teeth. For mouth, using red felt, cut out a square wide enough to fit under nose and down to chin. Round off corners. Stitch mouth under nose, using picture as a guide. Pin teeth into mouth; stitch into position. For eyes, cut out 2 small circles from white felt and pin into position. Secure to head with French knot in center in black 4-ply soft or other suitable yarn.

LEGS (make 2)

Using yarn MC & US 6 (4.00mm) needles, cast on 11 sts.

Row 1: Knit.
Row 2: Purl.
Row 3: K1, inc 1, knit to last sts, inc 1, k1 (13 sts)
Row 4: Purl.
Row 5: As Row 3. (15 sts)
Row 6: Purl.
Rows 7–12: Work in St st.
Row 13: As Row 3. (17 sts)
Rows 14–18: Work in St st.
Row 19: As Row 3. (19 sts)

Work 9 rows in St st.

Foot pad

Using yarn A and US 6 (4.00mm) needles, cast on 4 sts.

Row 1: Knit.
Row 2: Knit.
Row 3: K1, inc 1, knit to last st, inc 1, k1. (6 sts)
Rows 4–10: Work as Rows 2–3, until 12 sts.
Rows 11–15: Knit.
Row 16: K1, sl1, knit to last 3 sts, k2tog, k1. (10 sts)
Row 17: Knit.
Rep last 2 rows once more. (8 sts)
Bind off.

ARMS (make 2)

Using yarn A and US 6 (4.00mm) needles, cast on 7 sts.

Row 1: Knit.
Row 2: Purl.
Row 3: K1, inc1, knit to last sts, inc 1, k1. (9 sts)
Row 4: Purl.
Row 5: As Row 3, place markers at beg and end of row. (11 sts)
Row 6: Purl.
Rows 7–12: Work in St st, place markers at beg and end of last row.
Row 13: As Row 3. (13 sts)
Rows 14–17: Work in St st.
Row 18: As Row 3. (15 sts)

Rep Rows 14–18 once more. (17 sts)
Rows 24–26: Work in St st.
Row 27: As Row 3. (19 sts)
Row 28: K1, sl 2, k1, psso, knit to last 4 sts, k3tog, k1. (15 sts)
Row 29: Purl.
Rep last two rows until 7 sts.
Last row: Purl to end.
Bind off.

Hand Pad

Using yarn A and US 6 (4.00mm) needles, cast on 4 sts.

Row 1: Knit.
Row 2: Knit.
Row 3: K1, inc 1, knit to last st, inc 1, k1. (6 sts)
Rows 4–7: Knit.
Row 8: K1, sl1, k1, psso, knit to last 3 sts, k2tog, k1. (4 sts)
Rows 9–10: Knit. Bind off.

Finishing

Sew in all loose ends. Block and press pieces flat. Using mattress stitch or backstitch, stitch front and back body pieces tog, leaving top open to insert stuffing. Stitch arms and legs between stitch markers. Pin and stitch hand and feet pads into position. Insert stuffing into arms and legs. Stitch legs and arms to body. Pin and stitch head sides to main body; insert stuffing. Stitch to top of body. Using picture as guide, stitch ears to head.

Godzilla

Materials

DOLL

★ Kid Classic by Rowan, approx
153 yd/50g ball, (70% lambswool,
26% kid mohair, 4% nylon)
    1 ball in Battle 845 (MC)
    1 ball in Spruce 853 (A)
★ 4-ply Soft by Rowan, approx
191 yd/50g ball, (100% wool)
    1 ball in Black 383 (B)
★ Pair US 6 (4.00mm) needles
★ White felt
    8 x 8in (20 x 20cm)
★ Red felt
    4 x 4in (10 x 10cm)
★ Green felt
    4 x 4in (10 x 10cm)
★ Red, white, and green sewing
thread

Note: Use Godzilla chart in the
template section for knitting
reference.

Pattern

BODY

Right and Left Sides
Using yarn MC and US 6 (4.00mm)
needles and working from graph, knit
left and right sides in St st.

Undercarriage
Using yarn A and US 6 (4.00mm)
needles, cast on 7 sts.
Row 1: Knit.
Row 2: Knit.
Rep Rows 1 and 2 nine
more times (20 rows in
total). Place markers at
end of 10th row.
Row 21: K1, m1, knit to
last sts, m1, k1. (9 sts)
Row 22: Knit to end.

Rep last 2 rows until 15 sts.
Work a further 20 rows in garter stitch.
Next row: K1, k2tog, knit to last 3 sts,
k2togtbl, k1. (13 sts)
Work 13 more rows garter stitch.
Next row: K1, k2tog, knit to last 3 sts,
k2togtbl, k1 (11 sts)
Work 3 rows garter stitch.
Next row: K1, k2tog, knit to last 3 sts,
k2togtbl, k1. (9 sts)
Work 5 rows garter stitch.
Next row: K1, k2tog, knit to last 3 sts,
k2togtbl, k1. (7 sts)
Work 7 rows garter stitch.
Next row: K1, k2tog,
knit to last 3 sts,
k2togtbl, k1.
(5 sts)
Work 40 rows
garter stitch.
Next row: K1, sl2,
k1, psso, k1. (3
sts)
Bind off.

Real Name: GOJIRA
Hometown: TOKYO
Achievements: A MAD RAMPAGE IN TOKYO; GODZILLA ALSO
HAS A STAR ON THE HOLLYWOOD WALK OF FAME
Verdict: LIZARD KING ICON

LEGS *(make 2)*

Using yarn MC and US 6 (4.00mm)
needles, cast on 5 sts.

Row 1: Knit.

Row 2: Purl.

Row 3: K1, m1, knit to last st, m1, k1.
(7 sts)

Row 4: P1, m1, purl to last st, m1, p1.
(9 sts)

Row 5: K1, m1, knit to last st, m1, k1.
(11 sts)

Row 6: Purl.

Row 7: Knit.

Rows 8–9: As Rows 6 and 7.

Row 10: Purl.

Row 11: K1, m1, knit to last st, m1, k1.
Place marker at beg and end of row.
(13 sts)

Rows 12–16: Work in St st.

Row 17: *K2, m1; rep from * 5 times, K2.
(19 sts)

Row 18: Purl.

Rows 19–22: Work in St st.

Row 23: *K2, k2tog; rep from * 5 times,
K2. (13 sts)

Rows 24–27: Work in St st. Place marker
at beg and end of last row.

Rows 28–34: Knit.

Rows 35–36: Bind off 3 sts at the
beginning of the next 2 rows.

Row 37: *K3, turn (leave rem sts on
needle); rep from * twice, k3tog.

Rejoin yarn, k2, k2tog, turn, k3, turn, k3, turn, k3tog.

ARMS *(make 2)*

Using yarn MC and four US 6 (4.00mm) needles, cast on 5 sts.

Row 1: Knit.

Row 2: Purl.

Row 3: K1, m1, knit to last st, m1, k1. (7 sts)

Row 4: P1, m1, purl to last st, m1, p1. (9 sts)

Row 5: K1, m1, knit to last st, m1, k1. (11 sts)

Row 6: Purl.

Row 7: Knit.

Rows 8–9: As Rows 6 and 7.

Row 10: Purl.

Row 11: K1, m1, knit to last st, m1, k1. Place marker at beg and end of row. (13 sts)

Rows 12–15: Work in St st. Place marker at beg and end of last row.

Rows 16–22: Knit.

Rows 23–24: Bind off 3 sts at the beginning of the next 2 rows.

Row 25: *K3, turn (leave rem sts on needle); rep from * twice, k3tog. Rejoin yarn, k2, k2tog, turn, k3, turn, k3, turn, k3tog.

Making up

Sewing up, sew in all loose ends.

Sew edge of left and right sides of body together using mattress stitch or backstitch. Sew 2in (5cm) of tail together.

Pin undercarriage to main part of body, starting at top of neck and marker on undercarriage toward the tail.

Insert stuffing from mouth opening, use knitting needle or similar implement to get the stuffing up into the tail.

MOUTH

Using template, cut out mouth from red felt fabric.

Pin into position at mouth opening and using red thread, stitch into position.

Teeth

Using template, cut out teeth. Pin into position around mouth, starting at the back, taking them up and over mouth. Stitch to mouth.

Cut out 2 small white circles from white felt fabric, stitch to head, and work a French knot at the center.

FIN

Using yarn A and US 6 (4mm) needles, cast on 3 sts.

Pattern Repeat 1

Row 1: Knit.

Row 2: K2, m1, k1. (4 sts)

Row 3: Knit.

Row 4: K3, m1, k1. (5 sts)

Row 5: Knit.

Row 6: K4, m1, k1. (6 sts)

Row 7: Bind off 3 sts, knit to end.

Rep Rows 2 and 7 of Pattern Repeat 1 twice more.

Pattern Repeat 2

Row 1: Knit.

Row 2: K2, m1, k1. (4 sts)

Row 3: Knit.

Row 4: K3, m1, k1. (5 sts)

Row 5: Knit.

Row 6: K4, m1, k1. (6 sts)

Row 7: K5, m1, k1. (7 sts)

Row 8: Knit to end.

Row 9: K6, m1, k1. (8 sts)

Row 10: Bind off 5 sts, knit to end.

Rep Rows 2 and 10 of Pattern Repeat 2 three times and Rows 2 and 7 of Pattern Repeat 1 twice more; on last rep of Row 7, bind off all sts.

Pin into position along back seam.

Madonna

Materials

DOLL

★ Wool Cotton by Rowan, approx 122yd/50g ball (50% wool/50% cotton)
    1 ball in Ecru 900 (MC)
★ Pure Silk by Jaeger, approx 137yd/50g ball (100% silk)
    1 ball in Chalk 590 (C)
★ KidSilk Haze by Rowan, approx 229yd/25g ball (70% kid mohair/30% silk)
    1 ball in Pearl 590 (D)
★ Pair of US 3 (3.25mm) needles
★ Pair of US 6 (4.00mm) needles

VIRGIN OUTFIT

★ Cotton Glace by Rowan, approx 137yd/50g ball (100% cotton)
    1 ball in Bleached 726 (B)

★ 1yd of ¼ in (0.5cm) wide white satin ribbon
★ Approx 12in (30cm) broad white satin ribbon
★ 1yd of white netting
★ Sewing thread to match
★ One large snap fastener

CORSET OUTFIT

★ Cotton Glace by Rowan, approx 137yd/50g ball (100% cotton)
    1 ball in Peony 822 (A)

★ Square of black felt 8¾ x 8¾ in (22 x 22cm)
★ 1yd of ¼ in (0.5cm) wide pink satin ribbon
★ Two small snap fasteners

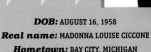

DOB: AUGUST 16, 1958
Real name: MADONNA LOUISE CICCONE
Hometown: BAY CITY, MICHIGAN
Achievements: "LIKE A VIRGIN," "LIKE A PRAYER," "RAY OF LIGHT," "MUSIC," AND "CONFESSIONS ON A DANCEFLOOR."
Verdict: ICONIC CHAMELEON

Pattern

DOLL

Using MC yarn, make a Basic Doll following the instructions on page 18.

Face

Using black thread, embroider face.
Eyes: French knots.
Mouth: Cut out heart/lip shape in red fabric and stitch into place.
Use backstitch to shape eyebrows.

Hair (make 2)

Using US 6 (4.00mm) needles and yarns C and D together, cast on 12 sts.
Rows 1–3: Knit.
Row 4: K8, turn.
Row 5: Knit.
Row 6: K4, turn.
Row 7: Knit.
Row 8: K8, turn.
Rows 9–13: Knit.
Row 14: K1, K2tog, knit to end. (11 sts)
Row 15: K to last 3 sts, k2tog, k1. (10 sts)
Row 16: Bind off 4 sts. (6 sts)
Rows 17–22: Knit.
Row 23: K6, cast on 4 sts at end of row. (10 sts)
Row 24: Knit.

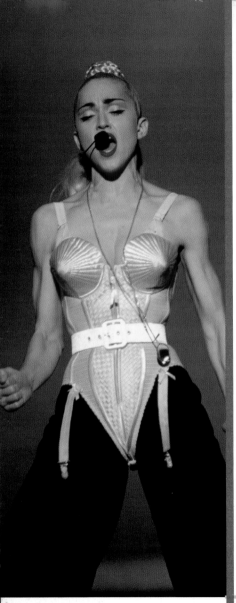

Row 25: Knit to last st, inc 1, k1.
(11 sts)
Row 26: K1, inc1, knit to end.
Row 27–29: Knit.
Row 30: K8, turn.
Row 31: Knit.
Row 32: K4, turn.
Row 33: Knit.
Row 34: K8, turn.
Rows 35–37: Knit.
Bind off.
Sew cast-on and bound-off edges tog.
With seam at center, sew top together.
Place on head and stitch into position.
Using yarn C and D together, cut 20
lengths approx 12in (30cm) long.
Taking approx 4 ends tog, fold in half;
using a crochet hook, pull through top
seam of hair and loop back on itself like
a tassel.
Work 4 at seam, 3 underneath, and 2
under again. Wrap a length of yarn
round top of tassels and secure in a
pony tail for one version. Cut to
required length using picture as guide.

VIRGIN OUTFIT
Corset
Front
Using US 3 (3.25mm) needles and yarn
B, cast on 6 sts.
Row 1: Knit to end.

Row 2: Purl to end.
Work 4 more rows in St st.
Row 7: K2, inc1, k2, inc1, k2. (8 sts)
Row 8: Purl to end.
Row 9: K3, inc1, k2, inc1, k3. (10 sts)
Row 10: Purl to end, cast on 5 sts.
(15 sts)
Row 11: K9, inc1, k2, inc1, k4, cast on
5 sts. (22 sts)
Row 12: K10, inc1, k2, inc1, k10.
Row 13: Purl to end.
Row 14: Knit to end.
Row 15: Purl to end.
Rows 16–24: Work in St st.
Cast off.
Back
Cast on 6 sts.
Row 1: Knit.
Row 2: Purl.
Work 4 more rows in St st.
Row 7: K2, m1, k2, m1, k2. (8 sts)
Row 8: Purl.
Row 9: K3, m1, k2, m1, k3. (10 sts)
Row 10: Purl to end, cast on 5 sts.
(15 sts)
Row 11: K9, m1, k2, m1, K4, cast on 5
sts. (22 sts)
Row 12: K10, m1, k2, m1, k10. (24 sts)
Row 13: Purl.
Row 14: Knit.
Row 15: Purl.
Row 16: K8, k3tog, yo, k1. Leave rem

sts on needle or slip on to stitch holder, turn. (11 sts)

Row 17: Purl.

Row 18: K7, k3tog, yo, k1.

Row 19: Purl.

Row 20: K6, k3tog, yo, k1.

Row 22: K5, k3tog, k1.

Row 24: K4, k3tog, yo, k1.

Row 25: Purl.

Row 26: Knit.

Bind off knitwise.

Rejoin yarn.

Row 1: K1, yfwd, sl 1, k2tog, psso, k8.

Row 3: K1, yfwd, sl 1, k2tog, psso, k7.

Row 5: K1, yfwd, sl 1, k2tog, psso, k6.

Row 7: K1, yfwd, sl 1, k2tog, psso, k5.

Row 9: K1, yfwd, sl 1, k2tog, psso, k4.

Row 10: Purl.

Row 11: Knit.

Bind off knitwise.

Sew in all loose ends.

Using mattress stitch, sew sides and bottom together.

Conical Bra

Using yarn B and US 3 (3.25mm) needles, cast on 16 sts.

Row 1: Knit.

Row 2: Purl.

Work Rows 1 and 2 twice more.

Row 7: *K3, ssk; rep from * twice more, k1. (13 sts)

Row 8: Purl.

Row 9: *K2, ssk; rep from * twice more, k1. (10 sts)
Row 10: Purl.
Row 11: *K1, ssk; rep from * twice more, k1. (7 sts)
Row 12: Purl.
Row 13: *Ssk; rep from * to end. (4 sts)
Break off yarn and thread through sts on needle. Pull tight and secure yarn; sew side seams together. Insert the required amount of stuffing. Pin into position on front of bodice and stitch.

Finishing

Sew up side seams.
Cut 2 lengths of ¼ in (0.5cm) ribbon in white and pink approx 1¾ in (4cm) long; pin and stitch straps to front and back. Cut 12in (30cm) of white and pink ¼ in (0.5cm) satin ribbon.
Starting at top thread ribbon, crisscross as shoe laces and tie at bottom.

Net Skirt

Cut 5 lengths approx 30 x 6in (80 x 15cm) and layer up on one and other.
Run 2 rows of tacking stitch quite close together through all 5 layers.
Pull these tight to gather fabric, to fit round waist of doll.
Pin broad ribbon to netting and stitch together; fold over ribbon and stitch to front of ribbon, sandwiching the netting in between.
Fold ends of ribbon to the inside of skirt and stitch. Sew snap fastener to ribbon.

Break off yarn and thread through sts on needle. Pull tight and secure yarn; sew side seams together. Insert required amount of stuffing. Pin into position on front of bodice and stitch. Cut two lengths of ¼ in (0.5cm) pink satin ribbon to 1¾ in (4cm).
Stitch to front of corset leg holes to create suspenders.
Stitch one half of snap fastener to ribbon.

Pants

Using template and black felt, cut out front and back of trousers (2 x E8). Pin WS together and stitch sides. Turn RS out.
With seam to the inside, fold in half. Stitch down fold close to the edge to create trouser crease. Sew other half of snap fastener to trousers.

PINK CORSET OUTFIT

Corset

Make the Front and Back as for the Corset instructions on page 60, using yarn A.

Conical Bra

Using yarn A and US 3 (3.25mm) needles, cast on 16 sts.

Row 1: Knit.
Row 2: Purl.
Row 3: *K3, ssk; rep from * twice, k1. (13 sts)
Row 4: P1, *p2tog tbl, p2; rep from * 3 times. (10 sts)
Row 5: *K1, ssk; rep from * twice, k1. (8 sts)

"Sometimes you have to be a bitch to get things done."

Andy Warhol

Materials

DOLL

* Wool Cotton by Rowan, approx 122yd/50g ball (50% wool/50% cotton)
    * 1 ball in Ecru 900 (MC)
* Pure Silk by Jaeger, approx 125yd/50g ball (100% silk)
    * 1 ball in Chalk 01 (A)
* KidSilk Haze by Rowan, approx 229yd/25g ball (70% kid mohair/30% silk)
    * 1 ball in Pearl 590 (B)
* Pair of US3 (3.25mm) needles and US 6 (4.00mm) needles
* Fiberfil
* Black embroidery thread

OUTFIT

* Cotton Glace by Rowan, approx 124yd/50g ball (100% cotton)
    * 1 ball in Black 727 (C)
* Square of black felt 8¾ x 8¾ in (22 x 22cm)
* Black embroidery thread
* One sewing needle

Pattern

DOLL

Using MC yarn, make a Basic Doll following the instructions on page 18.

Face

Using black thread, embroider face using picture as guide.
Eyes: French knots
Mouth and eyebrows: Backstitch

Hair

Using yarn A and B tog throughout, cast on 12 sts.

Rows 1–3: Knit.
Row 4: K8, turn.
Row 5: Knit.
Row 6: K4, turn.
Row 7: Knit.
Row 8: K8, turn.
Rows 9–13: Knit.
Row 14: K1, k2tog, knit to end. (11 sts)
Row 15: K to last 3 sts, k2tog, k1. (10 sts)
Row 16: Cast off 4 sts. (6 sts)
Rows 17–19: Knit.
Row 20: Bind off 2 sts at beg of row, knit to end. (4 sts).

DOB: AUGUST 6, 1928 **Died:** FEBRUARY 22, 1987
Real name: ANDREW WARHOLA
Hometown: PITTSBURGH, PENNSYLVANIA
Achievements: CAMPBELL'S SOUP CAN (1968); SHOT BLUE MARILYN (1964)
Verdict: POP ART ICON

Row 21: K4, cast on 2 sts. (6 sts)

Row 22: Knit.

Row 23: K6, cast on 4 sts at end of row. (10 sts)

Row 24: Knit.

Row 25: Knit to last st, m1, k1. (11 sts)

Row 26: K1, m1, knit to end.

Rows 27–29: Knit.

Row 30: K8, turn.

Row 31: Knit.

Row 32: K4, turn.

Row 33: Knit.

Row 34: K8, turn.

Rows 35–37: Knit.

Bind off.

Finishing

Sew cast-on and bound-off edges tog. With seam at center, sew top together. Place on head and stitch into position. Using yarn B only, cut 60 lengths approx 6in (15cm) long. Taking 3–4 strands at a time, fold in half; using a crochet hook, pull through front edge of hair and loop back on itself like a tassel. Cut to required length using picture as guide.

OUTFIT

Sweater

Back

Using US 3 (3.25mm) needles and yarn C, cast on 24 sts.

> # *"They always say time changes things, but you actually have to change them yourself."*

Row 1: Knit.

Row 2: Knit.

Row 3: Knit.

Row 4: Purl.

Work in St st for a further 12 rows as indicated in Rows 3 and 4, ending with a WS row.

Bind off 3 sts at beg of next 2 rows. (18 sts)

Work a further 7 rows in St st, ending with a knit row; bind off.

Front

Using US 3 (3.25mm) needles and yarn C, cast on 24 sts.

Row 1: Knit.

Row 2: Knit.

Row 3: Knit.

Row 4: Purl.

Work in St st for a further 12 rows as indicated in Rows 3 and 4, ending with a WS row. Bind off 3 sts at beg of next 2 rows. (18 sts)

Work a further 2 rows in St st.

Shape neck

Row 1: K7, turn.

Row 2: Purl.

Row 3: K4, k2tog, k1. (6 sts)

Row 4: P1, p2tog , purl to end. (5 sts)

Row 5: K1, k2tog, k1. (4 sts)

Bind off.

Rejoin yarn to center sts, cast off 4 sts, and knit to end.

Next row: Purl.

Next row: K1, ssk, knit to end. (6 sts)

Next row: P3, p2tog tbl, p1. (5 sts)

Next row: K1, ssk, knit to end. (4 sts)

Bind off.

Neck Band

Join right-hand shoulder together. With RS facing, pick up and knit 25 sts evenly around neck band. Work in 1 x 1 rib for 2 rows. Bind off in rib with US 6 (4.00mm) needles. Sew collar and shoulder up.

Sleeves

Using US 3 (3.25mm) needles, cast on

18 sts.

Row 1: Knit.

Row 2: Knit.

Row 3: Knit.

Row 4: Purl.

Work in St st until sleeve measures 3¼ in (8cm) or required length.

Shape top

Bind off 2 sts at beg of next row.

Row 1: K1, ssk, knit to last 3 sts, k2tog, k1. (16 sts)

Bind off.

Making Up

Sew in all loose ends. Sew sleeves into armhole. Sew up side seams and sleeves.

Pants

Using template, cut out front and back of pants (2 x E8). Pin WS together and stitch sides. Turn RS out.

Materials

DOLL

★ Wool Cotton by Rowan, approx
122yd/50g ball (50% wool/
50% cotton)
  1 ball in Antique 900 (MC)
★ Kid Classic by Rowan, approx
153 yd/50g ball (70% lambswool,
26% kid mohair, 4% nylon)
  1 ball in Smoke 831 (A)
★ 4-ply Soft by Rowan, approx
191 yd/50g ball (100% wool)
  1 ball in Black 383 (B)
★ Pair of US 6 (4.00mm) needles

OUTFIT

★ Piece of thick khaki cotton or old pair
of army pants
1yd (100cm)
★ Square red nylon felt
8¾ x 8¾ in (22 x 22cm)
★ Three hook and eyes
★ Sewing thread in black and red

"It's always darkest before it's totally black."

Chairman Mao

Pattern

DOLL

Using MC yarn, make a Basic Doll following the instructions on page 18.

Face

Embroider face on to head, using black yarn/embroidery thread. If using 4-ply Soft, split yarn down and use two strands together for eyes and 1 strand for mouth.

Eyes: French knots, with thread 4–5 times round needle.

Mouth: Backstitch.

Hair

Using US 6 (4.00mm needles) and yarn A, work as given for Gandhi's hair on page 76. Pin and stitch into position on head.

OUTFIT

Shirt

Using template, cut out front and back of shirt (2 x M3), collars (2 x M2), and button bands (2 x M4) from khaki fabric.

Button bands (make 2)

Using steam iron, fold up and press approx ⅜ in (1cm) in toward the center, then fold down rest of fabric in half, approx 1in (2.5cm) wide.

With folded edges to the RS, place shirt edge into folds of button band, pin, and stitch into position. Trim excess fabric. Place right sides of shirt back and front together and pin and stitch shoulders.

Cuffs (make 2)

Using steam iron, fold up and press approx ⅜ in (1cm) in toward the center, then fold down rest of fabric approx 1in (2.5cm). With folded edges to the RS, place cuff edge into folds of button band; pin and stitch into position. Fold sleeves in half, mark halfway point, and match up to shoulder seam.

With RS facing, pin and stitch.

Pin and stitch sleeve and side seams tog. Turn RS out and press all seams.

Collar

Using steam iron, fold up and press approx ⅜ in (1cm) in toward the center, then fold down rest of fabric in half, approx 1in (2.5cm) wide.

Pin and stitch to shirt.

Sew three hook and eyes to button band. Cut out 2 small rectangles from red felt to fit onto collar; pin and stitch as shown in photograph.

Pants

Using template, cut out front and back of trousers (2 x E8) from khaki fabric. Pin WS together and stitch sides. Turn RS out.

Hat

Work as given for Ringo's hat on page 72. Cut star from red fabric and sew onto front of hat.

DOB: DECEMBER 26, 1893
Died: SEPTEMBER 9, 1976
Real Name: MAO ZEDONG
Hometown: SHAOSHAN, XIANGTAN COUNTY, HUNAN PROVINCE

Achievements: CHAIRMAN OF THE COMMUNIST PARTY OF CHINA FROM 1945 TO 1976, 1ST PRESIDENT OF THE PEOPLE'S REPUBLIC OF CHINA FROM 1954 TO 1959.
Verdict: CULTURAL REVOLUTIONIST

The Beatles

Materials

* Wool Cotton by Rowan, approx 122yd/50g ball (50% wool/ 50% cotton)
    4 balls in Ecru 900 (MC)
* 4-ply Soft by Rowan, approx 191yd/50gm ball (100% merino wool)
    1 ball in Black 383 (D)
    1 ball in Expresso 389 (E)
* KidSilk Haze by Rowan, approx 229yd/25gm ball (70% kid mohair/ 30% silk)
    1 ball in Nightly 585 (F)
    1 ball in Villain 584 (G)
* Pair of US 3 (3.00mm) double pointed needles
* Pair of US 6 (4.00mm) needles

SGT PEPPER OUTFIT

* Scottish Tweed 4-ply by Rowan, approx 131yd/25gm ball (100% wool)
    1 ball in Gold 028 (A)
* Cotton Glace by Rowan, approx 124yd/50gm ball (100% cotton)
    1 ball in Peony 741 (B)
    1 ball in Bleached 726 (C)
* Squares pale blue, yellow, red, and pink felt
    10 x 10in (25 x 25cm)
* 12 snap fasteners
* Sewing thread to match fabrics

MOP TOP OUTFIT

* Squares white, yellow, gray, and black felt
    10 x 10in (25 x 25cm)
* Cotton Glace by Rowan, approx 124yd/50gm ball (100% cotton)
    1 ball in Poppy 741 (D)
* Twelve small gray buttons
* Sewing cotton to match fabric

Pattern

DOLLS

Using MC yarn, make 4 Basic Dolls following the instructions on page 18.

Faces

Using black thread, embroider faces using picture as guide.

Hair (make 4: one in yarns D and F, one in yarns E and F, two in yarns D and G tog)

Using US 6 (4.00mm) needles, cast on 12 sts.

Row 1: Purl.
Row 2: K2, inc 1, knit to last 3 sts, inc 1, k2. (14 sts)
Row 3: Purl.
Row 4: K2, inc 1, knit to last 3 sts, inc 1, k2. (16 sts)

John Lennon: OCTOBER 9, 1940–DECEMBER 8, 1980
Paul McCartney (JAMES PAUL MCCARTNEY): JUNE 18, 1942
George Harrison: FEBRUARY 25, 1943–NOVEMBER 29, 2001
Ringo Starr (NEE RICHARD STARKEY): JULY 7, 1940
Hometown: LIVERPOOL, ENGLAND

Achievements: THE BEST- SELLING MUSICAL ACT OF ALL TIME. IN THE UK, THE BEATLES RELEASED MORE THAN 40 BEST-SELLING SINGLES, AS WELL AS ALBUMS AND EPS THAT REACHED NUMBER ONE, INCLUDING "HELP," "YELLOW SUBMARINE," AND "ALL YOU NEED IS LOVE."
Verdict: FAB FOUR POP ICONS

Row 5: P2, inc 1, purl to last 3 sts, inc 1, p2. (18 sts)

Row 6: K2, inc 1, knit to last 3 sts, inc 1, k2. (20 sts)

Row 7: P2, inc 1, purl to last 3 sts, inc 1, p2. (22 sts)

Row 8: K2, inc 1, knit to last 3 sts, inc 1, k2. (24 sts)

Cast on 2 sts at the beginning of each row until 32 sts.

Row 13: Purl.

Row 14: *K2, k2tog; rep from * to end. (24 sts)

Row 15: Purl.

Row 16: *K1, k2tog; rep from * to end. (16 sts)

Row 17: Purl.

Row 18: [K2tog] rep to end. (8 sts)

Row 19: Purl.

Break off yarn, do not bind off; draw yarn through sts on needle and pull tight; secure yarn and sew seams tog. Place on basic doll head and stitch into position.

SGT PEPPER OUTFIT

Jackets *(make 1 in each color)*

Using templates, cut out front (2 x E3), back (E5), sleeves (2 x E4), and collar (E6).

Pin and sew shoulders tog. Pin sleeves into position, making sure center point of sleeve matches shoulder seam and sew tog. Pin and sew sides tog.

Pin and sew sleeves tog, leaving approx ½ in (1.5cm) at cuff opening.

Turn RS out. Pin and stitch collar into position.

Pants *(make 1 in each color)*

Using template, cut out front and back (2 x E7).

Pin WS together and stitch sides. Turn RS out.

Front Trims *(make 4: two sets of yellow, one set of red, and one set of white)*

Long eye cord (make 2 per jacket)

Using double-pointed needles, work eye cord as follows:

Cast on 4 sts.

Row 1: Knit.

Do not turn, but slide stitches to end of needle and knit; rep until cord measures approx 4¾in (12cm) or to fit front of jacket.

Bind off.

Short eye cord (make 3 per jacket)

Make three more eye cords, 12 rows each. With RS facing, pin long eye cords into position at front opening of jacket and stitch into position. Pin shorter eye cords into position across the front of jacket and stitch to the RS of jacket. Stitch one part of snap

fastener to end of eye cord, then stitch the other side to match up on jacket.

George's Pirate Hat

Using yarn B and US 3 (3.25mm) needles, cast on 8 sts.

Row 1: Purl.

Row 2: Knit into front and back of each st. (16 sts)

Row 3: Purl to end.

Row 4: Knit into front and back of each st. (32 sts)

Row 5: Purl.

Work a further 8 rows in St st.

Sew up side seam.

Hat Brim

Using template, cut out circular ring from red felt. Snip small cuts around inside ring toward outside ring as marked on template. Fold up snipped sections into inside of knitted hat and pin into position. Using matching thread, sew into position. Fold outside brim into 3 sections and stitch to outside of hat, using picture as a guide. Place feather on brim.

Ringo's Hat

Using template, cut out pieces from pink felt. Place right sides of circle and ring tog and, using backstitch, sew around outer edges. Turn right side out. Snip small cuts round the inside ring toward the outside ring as marked on template. Fold snipped sections up and pin and stitch black strip to snipped sections. Using template, cut out peak and stitch into position.

Drums

Bass Drum

Cut circle template from white fabric and all other templates from grey fabric. Allowing ⅛in (0.5cm) seams throughout, stitch ends of grey fabric together, then pin and stitch white circle to top. Repeat with Snare Drum and Low Tom.

Small and Large Cymbal

Cut circle templates from yellow fabric.

To make stands, using US 3 (3.25mm) needles and silver craft wire, cast on approx 150 stitches.
Bind off stitches to make a strip.
Fold over ⅓rd of wire and twist together.
With remaining length of wire, fold into 3 even sections to make the feet of the stand, leaving 2½ in (6.3cm) to wrap around feet and base to make secure.

Guitars and Bass

Cut out templates as indicated.
Sew front and back of guitar/bass body together. Pin and attach neck of guitar/bass to body. Pin and sew other sections to guitar using picture as guide.
For John's bass, sew front and back of bass head together, sew white motif to front. Sew bass head onto top of neck.

MOP TOP OUTFIT

Jackets *(make 4 in gray felt)*

Using templates, cut out front (2 x E2), back (E1), and sleeves (2 x E9).
Pin and sew shoulders tog. Pin sleeves into position, making sure center point of sleeve matches shoulder seam and sew tog. Pin and sew sides tog. Pin and sew sleeves tog. Turn RS out. Sew buttons onto front of jacket.

Pants *(make 4)*

Using template, cut out front and back (2 x E8) in gray felt.
Pin WS together and stitch sides. Turn RS out.

Shirts *(make 4 in white felt)*

Using templates, cut out front (H7), back (H6), and sleeves (H5). Pin and sew shoulders tog. Pin sleeves into position, making sure center point of sleeve matches shoulder seam, and sew tog. Pin and sew sides tog. Pin and sew sleeves tog. Turn RS out.
Fold collar in half and work a back stitch close to fold to create collar shape. Pin and stitch collar into position on body of shirt. Add buttons to front.

Ties *(make 4)*

Using yarn D and US 3 (3.25mm) needles, cast on 3 sts.
Rows 1–20: Knit.
Bind off.

Charlie Chaplin

Materials

- ★ Wool Cotton by Rowan, approx 122yd/50g ball (50% wool/ 50% cotton)
  - 1 ball in Ecru (MC)
- ★ Cotton Glace by Rowan, approx 124yd/50gm ball (100% cotton)
  - 1 ball in Black 727 (A)
- ★ 4-ply Soft by Rowan, approx 191yd/50g ball (100% merino wool)
  - 1 ball in Black 383 (B)
- ★ KidSilk Haze by Rowan, approx 229yd/25g ball (70% kid mohair, 30% silk)
  - 1 ball in Nightly 585 (C)
- ★ Pair of US 3 (3.25mm) and US 6 (4.00mm) needles
- ★ Fiberfill

- ★ Black embroidery thread

OUTFIT
- ★ Square of white felt 8¾ x 8¾ in (22 x 22cm)
- ★ Square of black felt 8¾ x 8¾ in (22 x 22cm)
- ★ Small piece of red felt
- ★ One snap fastener
- ★ Sewing thread to match fabric
- ★ One darning needle

DOB: APRIL 16, 1889
Died: DECEMBER 25, 1977
Real name: CHARLES SPENCER CHAPLIN, JR.
Hometown: LONDON, ENGLAND

Achievements: "THE TRAMP" IN *THE CIRCUS, CITY LIGHTS,* AND *MODERN TIMES*; "ADENOID HYNKEL" IN *THE GREAT DICTATOR*
Verdict: COMEDIC ICON

Pattern

DOLL
Using MC yarn, make a Basic Doll following the instructions on page 18.

Face
Using black thread, embroider face using picture on page 74 as guide.

Hair
Using US 6 (4.00mm) needles and yarns B and C together, cast on 12 sts.

Row 1: Knit to end.
Row 2: K2, m1, knit to last 3 sts, m1, k2. (14 sts)
Row 3: Knit to end.
Row 4: K2, m1, knit to last 3 sts, m1, k2. (16 sts)
Row 5: k2, m1, knit to last 3 sts, m1, p2. (18 sts)
Row 6: K2, m1, knit to last 3 sts, m1, k2. (20 sts)
Row 7: K2, m1, knit to last 3 sts, m1, p2. (22 sts)
Row 8: K2, m1, knit to last 3 sts, m1, k2. (24 sts)
Cast on 2 sts at the beginning of each row until 32 sts.

Row 13: Knit to end.

Row 14: *K2, k2tog; rep from * to end. (24 sts)

Row 15: Knit.

Row 16: *K1, k2tog; rep from * to end. (16 sts).

Row 17: Knit.

Row 18: [K2tog] rep to end. (8 sts)

Row 19: Knit.

Break off yarn, leaving a long tail; do not bind off. Draw yarn through stitches on needle and pull tight; secure yarn and sew seams tog. Place on basic doll head and stitch into position.

OUTFIT

Jacket

Using templates, cut out right and left front (2 x H1), back (H3), sleeves (2 x E9), and collar (H2) from black felt. Leave ¼ in (0.5cm) seam throughout. Pin and sew shoulders tog. Pin sleeves into position, making sure center point of sleeve matches shoulder seam, and sew together. Pin and sew sides tog. Pin and sew sleeves tog. Turn RS out. Fold collar in half and pin tog; stitch as close to edge as possible to create fold. Pin and stitch collar into position. Sew snap fastener to inside of jacket.

Shirt

Make as for The Beatles Shirt on page 72.

Pants (make 2)

Using US 3 (3.25mm) needles and yarn C, cast on 19 sts.

Row 1: Knit to end.

Row 2: Knit to end.

Work a further 2 rows in knit.

Row 7: K2, inc 1,*K2, inc 1; rep from * to last st, k1. (28 sts)

Row 8: Purl to end.

Row 9: Knit to end.

Work in St st for a further 7 rows, ending with a WS row.

Bind off 2 sts at beg of next 2 rows. (24 sts)

Continue working in St st until work measures approx 5in (12.5cm) from cast-on edge.

Next row: *K2, k2tog; rep from * to end.

Purl to end.

Bind off.

Sew front seams together; sew front and back crotch together; sew inside leg seams.

Hat

Using US 3 (3.25mm) needles and yarn A, cast on 8 sts.

Row 1: Purl.

Row 2: Knit into front and back of each stitch. (16 sts)

Row 3: Purl.

Row 4: Knit into front and back of each stitch. (32 sts)

Row 5: Purl.

Work a further 6 rows in St st.

Sew up side seam; let the fabric roll to create hat brim. Stuff lightly using fiberfill. Stitch into position on head.

Flower

Cut out small circle in red felt fabric; snip in toward center to create petals. Stitch into position on jacket lapel.

"Failure is unimportant. It takes courage to make a fool of yourself."

Materials

DOLL

★ Wool Cotton by Rowan, approx
122yd/50g ball (50% wool/50%
cotton)
  1 ball in Dream 929 (MC)
★ KidSilk Haze by Rowan, approx
229yd/25g ball (70% kid mohair,
30% silk)
  1 ball in Pearl 590 (A)
★ 4-ply Soft by Rowan, approx
191yd/50g ball (100% wool)
  1 ball in 383 (B)
★ Pair of US 6 (4.00mm) needles

OUTFIT

★ Piece of white cotton fabric approx
4 x 20in
(10 x 50cm)
★ White sewing
cotton
★ One reel silver
craft wire

Gandhi

Pattern

DOLL

Using MC yarn, make a Basic Doll
following the instructions on page 18.

Face

Embroider face on to head, using black
yarn/embroidery thread. If using 4-ply
Soft, split yarn down and use 2 strands
tog for eyes and 1 strand for mouth.
Eyes: French knot.
Mouth: Backstitch.
Pin and stitch glasses on to face using a
neutral shade of sewing cotton.

Hair

Using yarn and US 6 (4.00mm)
needles, cast on 3 sts.
Row 1: Knit to end.
Row 2: Knit to end.
Repeat last 2 rows 3 more times.
Row 9: K1, M1, knit to end.
Rows 10–14: Knit to end.
Row 15: K1, k2tog, knit to
end.
Rows 16–23: Knit to
end.
Bind off.

Sew in all loose ends and gently press
knitted fabric.
Pin to head and stitch into position,
using picture of doll as guide.

Glasses *(make 2)*

Wrap the craft wire approx 10 times
around a pencil, making a ring; break
off wire, leaving approx 8in (20cm)
length, and loop a couple of times
around the ring to secure.
Holding both rings approx ⅜ in (1cm)
apart, take one end of the wire and
thread through both rings 5 to 6 times
to form the bridge of the glasses.
Twist the bridge to secure; take the
ends of the wire and wrap around the
bridge and the rings.
Break off excess wire.

OUTFIT

Using the white cotton fabric, fold back
⅜ in (1cm) hem around edges and
stitch either by hand, using backstitch,
or by sewing machine.
Wrap fabric around waist of doll three
times to the back of the doll; take the
fabric between the legs and up over the
shoulder; and wrap around body and
tuck into the waist band.

DOB: OCTOBER 2, 1869
Death: JANUARY 30, 1948
Real Name: MOHANDAS
KARAMCHAND GANDHI
Hometown: PORBANDAR, INDIA
Achievements: PIONEER OF

SATYAGRAHA, THE RESISTANCE
OF TYRANNY FOUNDED UPON TOTAL
NON-VIOLENCE WHICH LED TO THE
INDEPENDENCE OF INDIA.
Verdict: PEACE-LOVING ICON

Queen Elizabeth II

Materials

DOLL

- ★ Wool Cotton by Rowan, approx 122yd/50gm ball (50% cotton/50% wool)
    - 1 ball in Antique 900 (MC)
- ★ 4-ply Soft by Rowan, approx 191yd/50g ball (100% merino wool)
    - 1 ball in Espresso 389 (A)
- ★ KidSilk Haze by Rowan, approx 229yd/25g ball (70% kid mohair/30% silk)
    - 1 ball in Villain 584 (B)
- ★ Pair of US 3 (3.25mm) and US 6 (4.00mm) needles

ROYAL COSTUME

- ★ Piece of white felt 8¾ x 8¾ in (22 x 22cm)
- ★ Piece of white netting 1yd x 5in (100cm x 12cm)
- ★ Small piece of pink felt or similar for mouth
- ★ Length of white broad satin ribbon 19¾ x 1¼ in (50 x 4cm)
- ★ Length of turquoise wired ribbon 19¾ x 1¼ in (50 x 4cm)
- ★ Approx 50 small clear beads
- ★ 1 spool platinum craft wire (0.28 weight)

DOB: APRIL 21, 1926
Hometown: LONDON, ENGLAND
Achievements: THE MONARCH OF THE ROYAL FAMILY; THE LARGEST LAND OWNER OF THE WORLD
Verdict: ROYAL ICON

Pattern

DOLL

Using MC yarn, make a Basic Doll following the instructions on page 18.

Face

Using black thread, embroider face, using picture as guide.

Eyes: French knots.

Mouth: Cut lip shape from pink felt fabric and stitch into place.

Eyebrows: Backstitch.

Hair

Using yarn A and B together throughout and using US6 (4.00mm) needles, cast on 14 sts.

Row 1: Knit.

Row 2: Knit.

Row 3: K2, m1, knit to last 2 sts, m1, k2. (16 sts)

Row 4: Knit.

Repeat rows 3 and 4 until 22 sts.

Next row: Cast on 18 sts and knit to end. (40 sts)

Next row: Knit.

Next row: *K2, k2tog; rep from * to end. (30 sts)

Next row: Knit.

Next row: *K1, k2tog; rep from * to end. (20 sts)

Next row: (P2tog), rep to end. (10 sts) Break off yarn, leaving approx 6in (15cm); thread through stitches on needle and pull tight; secure yarn and sew side tog. With front RS facing, pick up and knit 22 sts from side seam to cast-on edge; you will be picking up on the inside.

Right Hand Flick

Row 1: Knit.

Row 2: K2, ssk, knit to end. (21 sts)

Row 3: K1, k2tog, k12, slip next stitch onto RH needle, yarn forward between needles, turn and slip stitch back onto other needle, yarn back between needles ready to knit.

Row 4: K11, ssk, k1.

Row 5: K10, slip next stitch onto RH needle, yarn forward between needles, turn and slip stitch back onto other needle, yarn back between needles ready to knit.

Row 6: K7, sl1, k1, psso, k1.

Row 7: K8, slip next stitch onto RH needle, yarn forward between needles, turn and slip stitch back onto other needle, yarn back between needles ready to knit.

Row 8: K5, ssk, k1.

Bind off.

Turn back onto main part of hair and stitch ¾ in (2cm) along from side seam to cast-on edge.

Left Hand Flick

With front RS facing, pick up and knit 10 sts from cast-on edge to seam; you will be picking up with the purl side facing.

Row 1: Knit.

Row 2: K8, slip next stitch onto RH needle, yarn forward between needles, turn and slip stitch back onto other needle, yarn back between needles ready to knit.

Row 3: Knit to last 3 sts, k2tog, k1

Row 4: K6, slip next stitch onto RH needle, yarn forward between needles, turn and slip stitch back onto other needle, yarn back between needles ready to knit.

Row 5: Knit.

Row 6: K4, slip next stitch onto RH needle, yarn forward between needles, turn and slip stitch back onto other needle, yarn back between needles ready to knit.

Row 7: Knit.

Row 8: Knit.

Bind off.

Fold over and stitch into place. Place hair onto head and stitch into place.

ROYAL COSTUME

Dress

Using templates, cut out front (L1) and back (L2) from white felt. Leave ¼ in (0.5cm) seam throughout. Pin and sew shoulders tog. Pin and sew side seams tog. Stitch beads around neckline.

Net Skirt

Make as Madonna skirt on page 62, but do not fold over broad ribbon.

White Gloves

Make as Jackie O white gloves on page 33.

Crown

Using US 6 (4.00mm) needles and craft wire, cast on 100 sts.

Rows 1–3: Knit.

Bind off.

Wrap wire round pencil to create oval shapes as shown in the picture on page 79. Open out; using wire, stitch base of loops to stop unravelling.

Sew ends of wire together.

Stitch crown onto head.

Sash

Cut one length of turquoise wired ribbon long enough to wrap over one shoulder and across back and front (as in picture). Stitch ends together and drape over dress as shown.

Bob Marley

Materials

DOLL

- ★ Wool Cotton by Rowan, approx
  122yd/50g ball
  (50% wool/50% cotton)
  1 ball in Mocha 965(MC)
- ★ Kid Classic by Rowan, approx
  153yd/50g ball, (70% lambswool,
  26% kid mohair, 4% nylon)
  1 ball in Cherry Red 847 (B)
- ★ Biggy Print by Rowan, approx
  33yd/100g ball, (100% wool)
  1 ball in Savage 259 (C)
- ★ 4-ply Soft by Rowan, approx
  191yd/50g ball, (100% wool)
  1 ball in Black 383 (D)
- ★ Pair of US 6 (4.00mm) needles

OUTFIT

- ★ Length of mid-blue denim 100%
  cotton or old pair of jeans, approx
  1yd (100cm)
- ★ Two small snap fasteners
- ★ Four buttons
- ★ Black and white sewing cotton
- ★ Wool Cotton by Rowan, approx
  122yd/50g ball, (50% wool/
  50% cotton)
  1 ball in 908 (A)

Pattern

DOLL

Using MC yarn, make a Basic Doll
following the instructions on page 18.

Face

Using black thread, embroider face
using picture on page 82 as a guide.

Hair

Using yarn C, cut 14 lengths approx 8in
(20cm) long. Lay yarn out lengthways
next to one another; cut a long strip of
yarn D. Tie around center of first strip,
place next strip between yarn D, and tie
ends of yarn D tog. Rep this until all 14
strips of yarn are attached. Place
on head and
stitch down
center.

OUTFIT

Shirt

Using template, cut out front and back
(2 x P3), collars (2 x H4), sleeves (2 x
H5), button bands (2 x P1), and cuffs
(2 x P2) in denim. Leave ¼in (0.5cm)
seam throughout.

Button bands (make 2)

Using steam iron, fold up and press
approx ⅜in (1cm) in toward the center,
then fold down rest of fabric.
With folded edges to the right side,
place shirt edge into folds of button
band; pin and stitch
into position. Trim
excess fabric. Place
right sides of shirt
back and front
together and pin
and stitch
shoulders.

DOB: FEBRUARY 6, 1945
Died: MAY 11, 1981
Real Name: ROBERT NESTA MARLEY
Hometown: NINE MILES, SAINT ANN PARISH, JAMAICA
Achievements: POPULARIZED REGGAE. KNOWN FOR SUCH HITS AS "I SHOT THE SHERIFF," "NO WOMAN, NO CRY," "THREE LITTLE BIRDS," "EXODUS," "COULD YOU BE LOVED," "JAMMIN'" "REDEMPTION SONG," AND "ONE LOVE."
Verdict: REGGAE ICON

Cuffs (make 2)

Using steam iron, fold up and press approx ⅜ in (1cm) in toward the center, then fold down rest of fabric.

With folded edges to the right side, place cuff edge into folds of button band; pin and stitch into position. Fold sleeves in half, mark halfway point, and match up to shoulder seam. With RS facing, pin and stitch. Pin and stitch sleeve and side seams tog. Turn RS out and press all seams.

Collar

With RS tog, stitch along the sides and curved edge, leave straight edge open. Turn RS out, and use knitting needle or similar blunt point to poke out collar. Press using steam iron to flatten seams. Pin and stitch to shirt. Sew buttons to button band. Sew snap fastener onto button band.

Jeans

Using templates, cut out front and back (2 x P4). With RS tog, pin and stitch outer and inner side seams tog. Turn RS out and press fabric with steam iron. Fold in approx ⅜ in (1cm) hem at waist, and stitch. Fold in approx ⅜ in (1cm) hem at legs, and stitch.

Beanie

Using yarn A and US 6 (4.00mm) needles, cast on 8 sts.

Row 1: Purl to end.

Row 2: Knit into front and back of every st. (16 sts)

Row 3: Purl to end.

Row 4: As Row 2. (32 sts)

Rows 5–7: Work in St st.

Row 8: K2, m1. (42 sts)

Rows 9–11: Work in St st.

Row 12: K3, m1, knit to end. (52 sts)

Rows 13–15: Work in St st.

Row 16: *K3, k2tog; rep from * to end. (42 sts)

Rows 17–21: Work in St st.

Row 22: K2tog p1, k1: rep from * to end. (41 sts)

Row 23: *P1, k1; rep from * to end. Change to yarn B.

Row 24: *K1, p1; rep from * to end.

Row 25: As Row 23.

Change to yarn D.

Work in rib for 2 more rows.

Bind off.

Sew in all loose ends, sew up side seam and hat top.

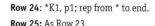

"Every man gotta right to decide his own destiny."

Audrey Hepburn

Materials

DOLL

★ Wool Cotton by Rowan, approx
122yd/50g ball (50% wool/
50% cotton)
    1 ball in Ecru 900 (MC)
★ Cotton Glace by Rowan, approx
127yd/50g ball (100% cotton)
    1 ball in Black 727 (A)
★ 4-ply Soft by Rowan, approx
191yd/50g ball (100% merino wool)
    1 ball in Espresso 389 (B)
★ KidSilk Haze by Rowan, approx
229yd/25g ball (70% kid mohair,
30% silk)
    1 ball in Villain 389 (C)
★ Pair of US 3 (3.25mm) needles

OUTFIT

★ Piece black felt
10 x 10in (25 x cm)
★ Small piece red felt fabric for lips
★ Black and red thread
★ One small snap fastener
★ One packet of clear small glass
beads
★ 50g reel of 0.20mm silver-plated
craft wire

Pattern

DOLL

Using MC yarn, make a Basic Doll
following the instructions on page 18.

Face

Cut out lip shape from red felt and
stitch onto face.
Embroider face on to head, using black
yarn/embroidery thread
If using 4-ply Soft, split yarn down and
use 2 strands tog for eyes and 1 strand
for mouth.
For eyes, French knot–wrap around
needle approx 4–5 times.

Hair

Using US 6
(4.00mm)
needle and
yarn B and C
held together,
cast on 12 sts.

Row 1: Knit to end.
Row 2: Purl to end.
Repeat rows 1 and 2 once more.
Row 5: K8, slip next stitch, yarn
forward, turn.
Row 6: Slip first stitch, purl to end.
Row 7: K4, slip next stitch, yarn
forward, turn.
Row 8: Slip first stitch, purl to end.
Row 9: K4, pick up wrap on next stitch,
place on left-hand needle and knit next
st and wrap together, k3 sts, slip next
stitch, yarn forward, turn.
Row 10: Slip first stitch, purl to end.
Rows 11–14: Work in St st.
Row 15: K1, sl1, k1, psso, knit to
end. (11 sts)
Row 16: K to last 3 sts, k2tog,
k1. (10 sts)
Row 17: Bind off 4 sts purlwise,
knit to end.
(6 sts)
Rows 18–26: Work in St st.
Cast on 4 sts at end of last
row. (10 sts)

DOB: MAY 4, 1929
Died: JANUARY 20, 1993
Real Name: AUDREY KATHLEEN RUSTON
Hometown: BRUSSELS, BELGIUM

Achievements: UNICEF GOODWILL
AMBASSADOR; "HOLLY GOLIGHTLY" IN
BREAKFAST AT TIFFANY'S; IMMORTALIZING
THE LITTLE BLACK DRESS
Verdict: FASHION ICON

Row 27: Knit to end.

Row 28: Purl to last st, M1, p1. (11 sts)

Row 29: K1, M1, knit to end. (12 sts)

Rows 30–34: Work in St st.

Row 35: K8, slip next stitch, yarn forward, turn.

Row 36: Slip first stitch, purl to end.

Row 37: K4, slip next stitch, yarn forward, turn.

Row 38: Slip first stitch, purl to end.

Row 39: K4, pick up wrap on next stitch, place on left-hand needle and knit next stitch and wrap together, k3 sts, slip next stitch, yarn forward, turn.

Row 40: Slip first stitch, purl to end.

Rows 41–43: Work in St st.

Bind off.

Sew cast-on and bind-off edges together.

With seam at center, sew top together.

Bun

Using US6 (4mm) needles and yarns B and C held together, cast on 8 sts.

Row 1: Purl to end.

Row 2: Knit into front and back of every stitch to end. (16 sts)

Row 3: Purl to end.

Row 4: Knit into front and back of every stitch to end. (32 sts)

Row 5: Knit to end.

Row 6: Purl to end.

Row 7: *K2tog, rep from * to end. (16 sts)

Row 8: Purl to end.

Row 10: As row 7. (8 sts)

Break off yarn and draw through stitches on needle and pull tight.

Sew up side seam; insert stuffing into bun.

Stitch bun center top of main hair.

Stitch hair into position on head.

OUTFIT

Dress

Using templates, cut out front and back (2 x A1) and waistband (A2) from black felt. Leave ¼ in (0.5cm) seam throughout.

Pin and sew shoulders together. Pin and sew sides together. Turn RS out.

Pin and stitch waistband to front only. Sew snap fastener onto back of waistband. Cut slit along front as shown in photo.

Gloves

Using US 3 (3.25mm) needles and yarn A, cast on 8 sts.

Row 1: Knit to end.

Row 2: Purl to end.

Row 3: K1, inc 1, knit to last sts, inc 1, k1. (10 sts)

Row 4: Purl to end.

Row 5: As row 3. (12 sts)

Row 6: Purl to end.

Work in St st for a further 10 rows or required length.

Bind off.

Tiara

Thread approx 20 beads onto craft wire.

Using US 6 (4.00mm) needles, cast on 40 sts.

Bind off as follows: K2 sts, bring first sts on left-hand needle up, over and off needle, *bring bead up and knit next st, bring first sts on left-hand needle up, over, and off needle, K1, rep from * to end.

Break off wire, leaving approx 4in (10cm) at end.

Twist approx 4 peaks into wire, using photo on page 84 as reference.

Place around bun with peaks to the front, tie ends of yarn together, and trim wire as needed.

Necklace

Thread approx 40 beads onto craft wire.

Using US6 (4.00mm) needles, cast on 40 sts.

Bind off as follows: K2 sts, bring first sts on left-hand needle up, over, and off needle, * bring bead up and knit next st, bring first sts on left-hand needle up, over, and off needle, K1, rep from * to end.

Break off wire, leaving approx 10cm at end. Wrap around neck and tie ends together at back; trim wire as needed.

Bob Dylan

Materials

DOLL

* Wool Cotton by Rowan, approx 122yd/50g ball (50% wool/50% cotton)
    * 1 ball in Ecru 900 (MC)
* Kid Silk Haze by Rowan, approx 229yd/25g ball (70% kid mohair/ 30% silk)
    * 1 ball in Villain 584 (A)
* 4-ply Soft by Rowan, approx 191yd/50g ball (100% wool)
    * 1 ball in Black 383 (B)
* Pair of US 3 (3.25mm) needles

OUTFIT

* Piece of white cotton 5 x 5in (12.5 x 12.5cm)
* Square of black denim 5 x 5in (12.5 x 12.5cm)
* Square of black felt 5 x 5in (12.5 x 12.5cm)
* One small snap fastener
* Three buttons
* Black and white thread

Pattern

DOLL

Using MC yarn, make a Basic Doll following the instructions on page 18.

Face

Embroider face on to head, using black yarn/embroidery thread. If using 4-ply Soft, split yarn down and use 2 strands together for eyes and 1 strand for mouth.

Eyes: French knot, thread 4–5 times round needle.

Mouth: Backstitch.

Hair

Special abbreviation: L1 = loop 1: Insert knit wise needle into next stitch, bring first finger on left hand under the RH needle, take yarn over needle and under finger twice, take yarn over and under needle; do not take finger out of loops; pull all 3 loops on RH needle back through stitch on LH needle and slip LH stitch off needle; slip 3 loops back onto LH needle and knit as normal. It is important to keep finger in the loops until knitted.

Using US 3 (3.25mm) needles and yarns A and B together, cast on 11 sts.

Row 1: Knit to end.

DOB: JANUARY 19, 1946
Real Name: ROBERT ALLEN ZIMMERMAN
Hometown: DULUTH, MINNESOTA
Achievements: AWARD-WINNING

AMERICAN SINGER-SONGWRITER, AUTHOR, AND MUSICIAN KNOWN FOR HITS SUCH AS "MR. TAMBOURINE MAN" AND "I WANT YOU."
Verdict: SONGWRITING ICON

Row 2: K1, *L1, k1, rep from * to end.
Row 3: K1, m1, k to last st, m1, k1. (13 sts)
Rep last 2 rows until 19 sts.
Row 9: Knit to end.
Row 10: K2,* L1, k1, rep from * to last st, k1.
Row 11: Knit to end.
Row 12: K1, *L1, k1; rep from * to end.
Row 13: Bind off 3 sts at beg of row, knit to end. (16 sts)
Row 14: Bind off 3 sts, K1, *L1, k1, rep from * to end. (13 st)
Row 15: K1, ssk, k to 3 sts, k2tog, k1. (11 sts)
Row 16: K1, *L1, k1, rep from * to end.
Repeat rows 15–16 until you have 9 sts.
Next row: Knit to end.
When working loop sts on next row, work yarn round 2 fingers to make loop longer.
Next row: K2, *L1, k1, rep from * to last st, k1.
Bind off.
Sew in all loose ends, pin hair to head, and stitch into position.

"I'm the spokesman for a generation."

OUTFIT

Shirt

Using template, cut out front and back (2 x P3), collars (2 x H4), sleeves (2 x H5), button bands (2 x P1), and cuffs (2 x P2) in denim. Leave ¼ in (0.5cm) seam throughout.

Button bands (make 2)

Using steam iron, fold up and press approx ⅜ in (1cm) in toward the center, then fold down rest of fabric.

With folded edges to the RS, place shirt edge into folds of button band; pin and stitch into position. Trim excess fabric. Place RS of shirt back and front together; pin and stitch shoulders.

Cuffs (make 2)

Using steam iron, fold up and press approx ⅜ in (1cm) toward the center, then fold down rest of fabric.

With folded edges to the RS, place cuff edge into folds of button band; pin and stitch into position.

Fold sleeves in half, mark halfway point, and match up to shoulder seam. With RS facing, pin and stitch,

Pin and stitch sleeve and side seams together.

Turn RS out and press all seams.

Collar

With right sides together, stitch along the sides and curved edge; leave straight edge open.

Turn right sides out, and use knitting needle or similar blunt point to poke out collar.

Press using steam iron to flatten seams. Pin and stitch to shirt.

Sew buttons to button band.

Sew snap fastener onto button band.

Jeans

Using templates, cut out front and back of jeans.

With RS together, pin and stitch outer and inner side seams together.

Turn RS out and press fabric with stream iron.

Fold in approx ⅜ in (1cm) hem at waist and stitch.

Fold in approx ⅜ in (1cm) hem at legs and stitch.

Vest

Using template, cut out back (Q3) and front (2 x Q4) from black fabric.

Sew shoulders together.

Sew side seams together, leaving approx 1⅜ in (4cm) opening at top for armhole.

Turn RS out and press with cool iron.

Cowboy Hat

Using yarn B, work top as for George Harrison's pirate hat brim on page 72. Using template, cut out a ring (P5) from black felt.

Stitch to inside as given for George Harrison's pirate hat; fold sides up and stitch into position.

Mr T

Materials

DOLL

- ★ Wool Cotton by Rowan, approx 122yd/50g ball (50% wool/50% cotton)
  - 1 ball in Mocha 965(MC)
- ★ Kid Classic by Rowan, approx 153yd/50g ball (70% lambswool, 26% kid mohair, 4% nylon)
  - 1 ball in Smoke 831 (A)
- ★ 4-ply Soft by Rowan, approx 191yds/ 50g ball (100% wool)
  - 1 ball in Black 383 (B)
- ★ Pair of US 6 (4.00mm)

OUTFIT

- ★ Blue denim fabric (or old pair of jeans)
  - 20 x 20in (50 x 50cm)
- ★ Small piece of red felt for epaulets
- ★ 1 x reel (175m) 0.200mm, craft wire champagne/gold
- ★ 1 x small snap fastener
- ★ Black and red sewing thread

Pattern

DOLL

Using MC yarn, make a Basic Doll following the instructions on page 18.

Face

Embroider face on to head, using black yarn/embroidery thread.

If using 4-ply soft, split yarn down and use 2 strands tog for eyes and 1 strand for eyebrows.

Eyes: French knot–wrap yarn around needle approx 4–5 times.

Eyebrows: Backstitch.

Beard: Work as given for Abraham Lincoln on page 29, using US 6 (4.00mm) needles and Kid Classic yarn.

Hair

Special abbreviation L1 = loop 1:

Insert knit wise needle into next stitch, bring first finger on left hand under the RH needle; take yarn over the needle and under finger twice, take yarn over and under needle; do not take finger out of the loops; pull all 3 loops on RH needle back through stitch on LH needle and slip stitch off needle; slip 3 loops back onto LH needle and knit as normal. Keep finger in the loops until knitted.

Using US 6 (4.00mm) needles and Kid Classic yarn, cast on 7 sts.

Row 1: Knit.

Row 2: K1,* L1, K1, rep from * to end.

Row 3: Knit.

Row 4: K2, *L1, K1, rep from * to end.

Repeat rows 1–4 3 more times and rows 1 once more. Bind off.

DOB: MAY 21, 1952
Real Name: LAURENCE TUREAUD
Hometown: CHICAGO, ILLINOIS
Achievements: ACHIEVED FAME FOR HIS ROLES AS SERGEANT B. A. BARACUS

IN *THE A-TEAM*, BOXER CLUBBER LANG IN THE 1982 FILM *ROCKY III*, AND FOR HIS NUMEROUS APPEARANCES IN THE WWF.
Verdict: ICON WHO PITIES THE FOOL

" I'm teaching fools some basic rules."

OUTFIT

Shirt

Using template, cut out front and back (2 x B1), collars (2 x M2) and button bands (2 x M4), and epaulets (2 x B3) in denim. Leave ¼ in (0.5cm) seam throughout.

Button bands (make 2)

Using steam iron, fold up and press approx ⅜ in (1cm) toward the center, then fold down rest of fabric.

With folded edges to the RS, place shirt edge into folds of button band; pin and stitch into position. Trim excess fabric. Pin RS of shirt back and front together; pin and sew shoulders.

Mark fabric approx 2in (5cm) up from bottom at the sides to mark bottom of armhole.

Pin and sew side seams together, between the bottom and armhole mark.

Turn RS out and press all seams.

Collar

With RS together, stitch along the sides and curved edge; leave straight edge open.

Turn RS out, and use knitting needle or similar blunt point to poke out collar. Press to flatten seams.

Pin and stitch to shirt.

Front embellishment

Using template, cut out 2 front panels in red felt.

Pin and stitch onto shirt front, using picture on page 90 as guide.

Sew snap fastener onto button band.

Finishing

Pin hair onto top of head and stitch into position.

Pin beard on to face and stitch into position.

Using yarn A, stitch mustache onto face, using picture on page 90 as guide.

Jeans

Using templates, cut out front and back (2 x B2) in denim. Leave ¼ in (0.5cm) seam throughout.

With RS together, pin and stitch outer and inner side seams together.

Turn RS out and press fabric with stream iron.

Fold in approx ⅜ in (1cm) at waist, and stitch.

Chains

Using US 6 (4.00mm) needles and craft wire, cast on 2 sts, *take first stitch and pass over 2nd stitch, cast on 1 st, rep from * to required length, approx 70 sts.

David Bowie

Materials

DOLL

* Wool Cotton by Rowan, approx 122yd/50g ball (50% wool/50% cotton)
    1 ball in Antique 900 (MC)
* Tapestry by Rowan, approx 131yd/50g ball (70% wool, 30% soya bean)
    1 ball in Antique 173 (A)
* KidSilk Haze by Rowan, approx 229yd/25g ball (70% kid mohair, 30% silk)
    1 ball in Marmalade 596 (B)
* Pair of US6 (4.00mm) needles
* Fiberfill
* Black embroidery thread
* One embroidery needle

OUTFIT

* Piece of white felt
    8¾ x 8¾ in (22 x 22cm)
* Piece of red, green, and gold felt
    Each 6 x 1¾ in (15 x 4.5cm)
* Piece of pink felt
    1¾ x 1in (4cm x 2.5cm)
* Scrap of pink transparent fabric
* Matching threads
* Small amount of blue, pink, and green embroidery thread

DOB: JANUARY 8, 1947
Real name: DAVID ROBERT JONES
Hometown: LONDON, ENGLAND
Achievements: HUNKY DORY; THE RISE AND FALL OF ZIGGY STARDUST AND THE SPIDERS FROM MARS; ALADDIN SANE; LET'S DANCE
Verdict: GLAM ROCK ICON

Pattern

DOLL

Using MC yarn, make a Basic Doll following the instructions on page 18.

Face

Embroider face on to head, using blue and green embroidery thread for eyes. Backstitch smile with pink thread. Stitch lightning bolt to face, using picture on page 94 as reference.

Hair

Using yarn A and B together throughout and US6 (4mm) needles, cast on 12 sts.

Rows 1–3: Knit.
Row 4: K8, turn.
Row 5: Knit.
Row 6: K4, turn.
Row 7: Knit.
Row 8: K8, turn.
Rows 9–13: Knit.
Row 14: K1, K2tog, knit to end. (11 sts)
Row 15: K to last 3 sts, k2tog, k1. (10 sts)
Row 16: Bind off 4 sts. (6 sts)
Rows 17–19: Knit.
Row 20: Bind off 2 sts at beg of row, knit to end. (4 sts)
Row 21: K4, cast on 2 sts. (6 sts)

Row 22: Knit.

Row 23: K6, cast on 4 sts at end of row. (10 sts)

Row 24: Knit.

Row 25: Knit to last st, m1, k1. (11 sts)

Row 26: K1, m1, knit to end. (12 sts)

Rows 27–29: Knit.

Row 30: K8, turn.

Row 31: Knit.

Row 32: K4, turn.

Row 33: Knit.

Row 34: K8, turn.

Rows 35–37: Knit.

Bind off.

Sew cast-on and bound-off edges tog. With seam at center, sew top together. Place on head and stitch into position. Using yarn B, cut 60 lengths approx 8in (20cm) long.

Taking 3–4 strands at a time, fold in half, and using a crochet hook, pull through front edge of hair loop back on itself like a tassel. Work tassels through hairline, front, back, and sides. Flick back hair from front and stitch to main part of hair.

Style and cut to required length using picture as guide.

OUTFIT

Jumpsuit

Using templates, cut out front and back (2 x G1), sleeves (E9) in white felt, and shoulder epaulets (2 x E10) and collar (2 x E6) in gold.

Cut out thin strips of red and green felt approx ¼ in (0.5mm) wide as shown in the picture.

Leave ¼ in (0.5cm) seam throughout. Sew colored strips to front, back, and sleeves in alternate green and red.

Pin and sew shoulders together.

Pin sleeves into position, making sure center point of sleeve matches shoulder seam, and sew together.

Pin and sew sides together.

Pin and sew sleeves together.

Pin and sew inside legs together.

Turn RS out.

Using backstitch, sew collar on to jumpsuit.

Pin and stitch epaulets to top of shoulders.

Elvis

Materials

DOLL

★ Wool Cotton by Rowan, approx 122yd/50g ball (50% wool/ 50% cotton)
    1 ball in Dream 929 (MC)
★ Scraps of 4-ply cotton in black
★ Pair of US 3 (3.25mm) needles
★ Fiberfill
★ Scrap of embroidery thread in black

JUMPSUIT OUTFIT

★ Cotton Glace by Rowan, approx 124yd/50g ball (100% cotton)
    Scrap of White (A)
★ Scrap of DK cotton in gold
★ White felt 10 x 10in (25 x 25cm)
★ 23 blue sequins
★ 23 green beads

JAILHOUSE ROCK

★ Cotton Glace by Rowan, approx 124yd/50g ball (100% cotton)
    Scrap of White (A) and Black (B)
★ Piece of denim or old pair of jeans
★ Small shirt buttons in white
★ Brown and white thread

Pattern

DOLL

Using MC yarn, make a Basic Doll following the instructions on page 18.

Face

Use leftover black yarn to make eyes. Embroider a mouth, making it slightly wider on one side.

Hair

Using US US6 (4mm) needles and yarns A and B tog throughout, cast on 10 sts.

Row 1: Knit to end.
Row 2: Knit to end.
Row 3: K2, inc 1, k to last 2 sts, inc 1, k2. (12 sts)
Row 4: Knit.
Repeat Rows 2 and 3 until 18 sts.
Row 11: Knit to end.
Row 12: Purl to end.
Rows 13–14: Cast off

3 sts at beg of next 2 rows. (12 sts)
Row 15: K1, s11, k1, psso, k to last 3 sts, k2tog, k1. (10 sts)
Row 16: Purl to end.
Repeat rows 15–16 until 4 sts.
Work a further 7 rows keeping St st sequence correct.
Cast off.
Turn back 4 sts onto main fabric and stitch slightly to the left to create quiff.

JUMPSUIT OUTFIT

Jumpsuit

Using template, cut out front and back (2 x G1), collar (2 x Q1), cuffs (2 x Q2), and flares (2 x Q3) from white felt. Leave ¼in (0.5cm) seam throughout.

Fold back front opening edges of jumpsuit to create a deep V and pin. Stitch into place. Fold back bottom edge of trouser legs and stitch to create a hem. Stitch together shoulder seams of front and back pieces. Fold back opening

DOB: JANUARY 8, 1935 **Died:** AUGUST 16, 1977
Real name: ELVIS AARON PRESLEY
Hometown: MEMPHIS, TENNESSEE
Achievements: SOLD OVER ONE BILLION RECORD UNITS WORLDWIDE, EARNED 14 GRAMMY NOMINATIONS, STARRED IN 31 FEATURE FILMS.
Verdict: THE KING OF ICONS

edge of sleeves and stitch to create a hem. Fold sleeve in half with RS tog and stitch into body of jumpsuit. Pin and stitch front and back pieces tog leaving 2in (5cm) opening at bottom of leg and 1⅜in (4cm) opening at bottom of sleeves.

Stitch 4 beads and sequins along open side of sleeve side seam. Stitch 5 beads and sequins along open edge of trouser side seams.

Belt

Using US 3 (3.25mm) needles and yarn A, cast on 7 sts.

Knit 10 rows in St st.

Next row: Knit 6 sts, inc 1, k1. (8 sts)

Work 3 rows in St st.

Next row: Knit 7 sts, inc 1, k1. (9 sts)

Work 3 rows in St st.

Next row: K7, k2tog, k1. (8 sts)

Work 10 rows St st.

Bind off.

Neckband

Using US 3 (3.25mm) needles and yarn A, cast on 5 sts.

Work in St st until strip is long enough to fit round front opening of jumpsuit. Place sequins and embroidery along belt and neckband using picture as a guide.

JAILHOUSE ROCK

T-shirt body *(make 2)*

Using US 3 (3.25mm) needles and yarn A, cast on 22 sts.

Rows 1–3: Knit to end.

Row 4: Purl to end.

Join in yarn B.

Row 5: Knit to end

Row 6: Purl to end.

Change to yarn A.

Row 7: Knit to end.

Row 8: Purl to end.

Rep Rows 5–8 once more and Rows 5–6 again.

Keeping stripe sequence correct, bind off 2 sts at beg of next two rows. (18 sts)

Work 2 rows in yarn A and 2 rows in yarn B.

Work one row in yarn A.

Bind off knitwise.

Sew shoulders together, taking 4 sts from front and back either side.

Sleeves *(make 2)*

Using US 3 (3.25mm) needles and yarn A, with RS facing, pick up and knit 15 sts evenly around armhole.

Work 2 rows in St st.

Bind off knitwise.

Jacket

Using templates, cut front (2 x E2), back (E1), sleeves (2 x E9), and collar (H4) from denim. Leave ¼ in (0.5cm) seam throughout.

Pin together and stitch front and back shoulders together. Pin together and stitch sleeves into armholes.

Pin together and stitch side seams together. Turn RS out. Fold edgings in half lengthwise and press.

Pin into position around edge of jacket and stitch into place. Using white thread, topstitch ⅜ in (1cm) from front edge and hems. Roll cuffs over.

Pants

Using template and denim fabric, cut out front and back of trousers (2 x E8). Pin WS together and stitch sides. Turn RS out. Using white thread, stitch ⅜ in (1cm) along front and hem. Sew on buttons along front.

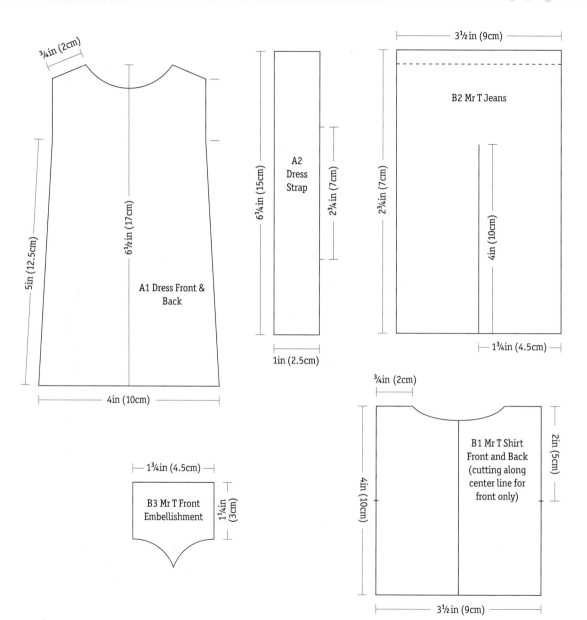

¾in (2cm)

A1 Dress Front & Back

6½in (17cm)

5in (12.5cm)

4in (10cm)

A2 Dress Strap

6¼in (15cm)

2¾in (7cm)

1in (2.5cm)

3½in (9cm)

B2 Mr T Jeans

2¾in (7cm)

4in (10cm)

1¾in (4.5cm)

B3 Mr T Front Embellishment

1¾in (4.5cm)

1¼in (3cm)

¾in (2cm)

B1 Mr T Shirt Front and Back (cutting along center line for front only)

4in (10cm)

2in (5cm)

3½in (9cm)

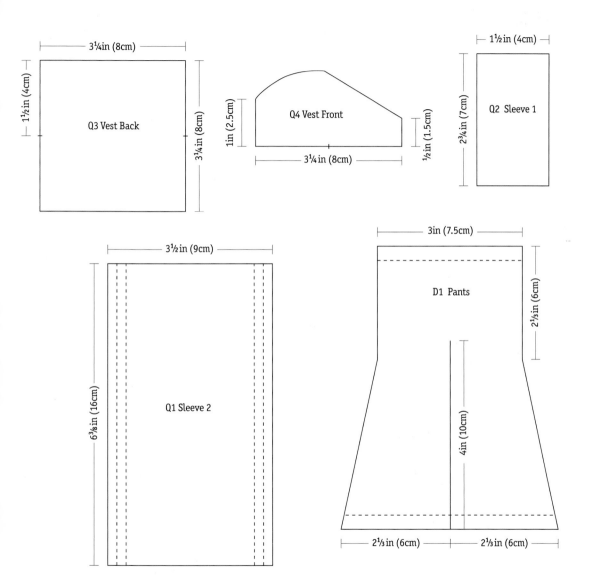

3¼in (8cm)

1½in (4cm)

Q3 Vest Back

3¼in (8cm)

1in (2.5cm)

Q4 Vest Front

3¼in (8cm)

½in (1.5cm)

1½in (4cm)

Q2 Sleeve 1

2¾in (7cm)

3½in (9cm)

6⅜in (16cm)

Q1 Sleeve 2

3in (7.5cm)

D1 Pants

2⅓in (6cm)

4in (10cm)

2⅓in (6cm)

2⅓in (6cm)

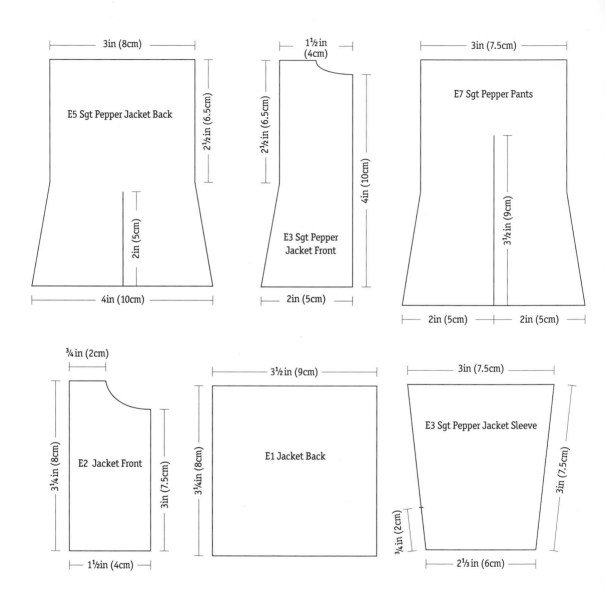

3in (8cm)

E5 Sgt Pepper Jacket Back

2½in (6.5cm)

2in (5cm)

4in (10cm)

1½in (4cm)

2½in (6.5cm)

E3 Sgt Pepper Jacket Front

4in (10cm)

2in (5cm)

3in (7.5cm)

E7 Sgt Pepper Pants

3½in (9cm)

2in (5cm)

2in (5cm)

¾in (2cm)

3¼in (8cm)

E2 Jacket Front

3in (7.5cm)

1½in (4cm)

3½in (9cm)

3¼in (8cm)

E1 Jacket Back

3in (7.5cm)

E3 Sgt Pepper Jacket Sleeve

3in (7.5cm)

¾in (2cm)

2⅓in (6cm)

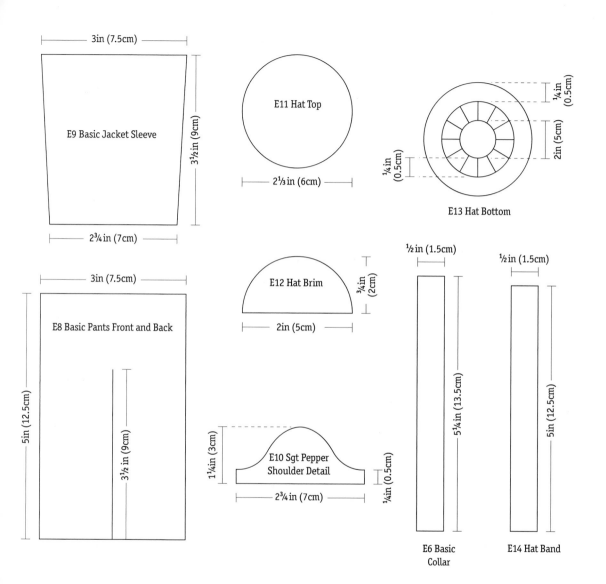

3in (7.5cm)

E9 Basic Jacket Sleeve

3½in (9cm)

2¾in (7cm)

E11 Hat Top

2⅓in (6cm)

¼in (0.5cm)

2in (5cm)

¼in (0.5cm)

E13 Hat Bottom

3in (7.5cm)

E8 Basic Pants Front and Back

5in (12.5cm)

3½in (9cm)

E12 Hat Brim

¾in (2cm)

2in (5cm)

½in (1.5cm)

½in (1.5cm)

E10 Sgt Pepper Shoulder Detail

1¼in (3cm)

¼in (0.5cm)

2¾in (7cm)

5¼in (13.5cm)

5in (12.5cm)

E6 Basic Collar

E14 Hat Band

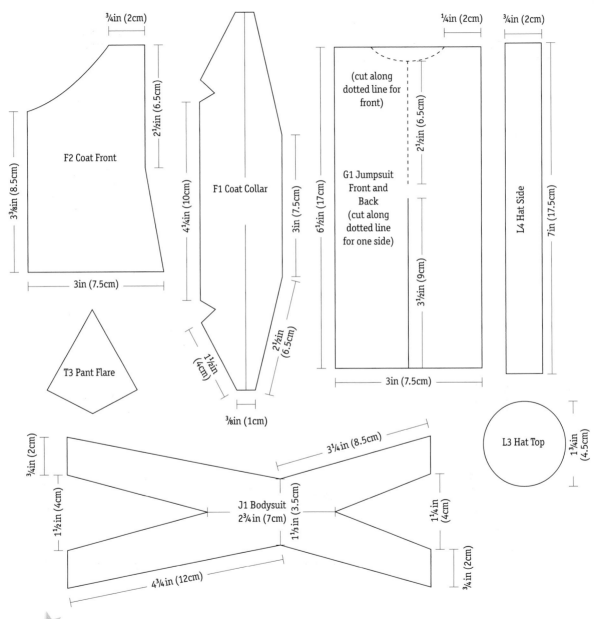

¾in (2cm)

2½in (6.5cm)

F2 Coat Front

3⅜in (8.5cm)

3in (7.5cm)

F1 Coat Collar

4¼in (10cm)

3in (7.5cm)

2½in (6.5cm)

1½in (4cm)

⅜in (1cm)

T3 Pant Flare

¼in (2cm)

¾in (2cm)

(cut along dotted line for front)

2½in (6.5cm)

G1 Jumpsuit Front and Back (cut along dotted line for one side)

6½in (17cm)

3½in (9cm)

3in (7.5cm)

L4 Hat Side

7in (17.5cm)

L3 Hat Top

1¾in (4.5cm)

¾in (2cm)

1½in (4cm)

3¼in (8.5cm)

1⅓in (3.5cm)

J1 Bodysuit
2¾in (7cm)

1¼in (4cm)

¾in (2cm)

4¾in (12cm)

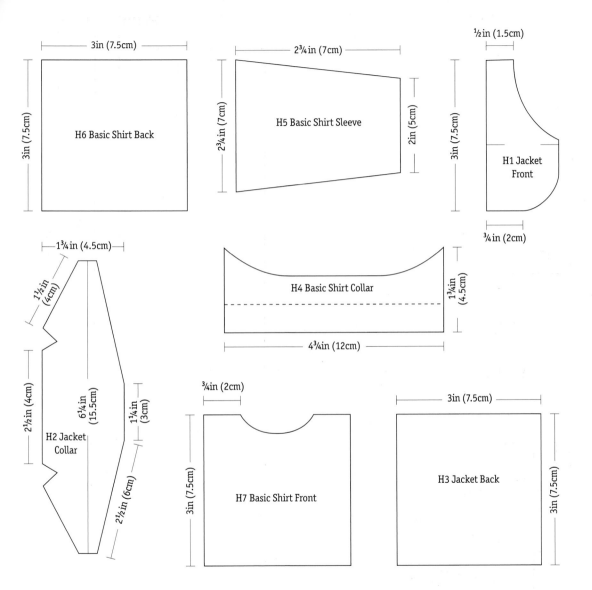

3in (7.5cm)

3in (7.5cm)

H6 Basic Shirt Back

2¾in (7cm)

2¾in (7cm)

2in (5cm)

H5 Basic Shirt Sleeve

½in (1.5cm)

3in (7.5cm)

H1 Jacket Front

¾in (2cm)

1¾in (4.5cm)

1½in (4cm)

2½in (4cm)

6¼in (15.5cm)

1¼in (3cm)

H2 Jacket Collar

2½in (6cm)

H4 Basic Shirt Collar

1¾in (4.5cm)

4¾in (12cm)

¾in (2cm)

3in (7.5cm)

H7 Basic Shirt Front

3in (7.5cm)

H3 Jacket Back

3in (7.5cm)

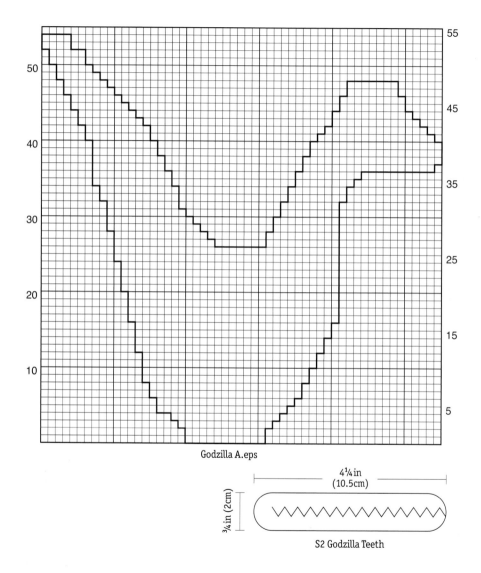

Godzilla A.eps

4¼ in
(10.5cm)

¾ in (2cm)

S2 Godzilla Teeth

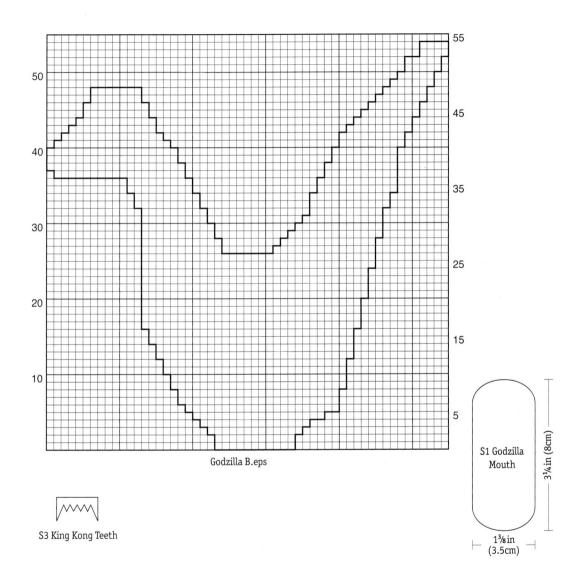

Godzilla B.eps

S3 King Kong Teeth

S1 Godzilla Mouth

3¼ in (8cm)

1⅜ in (3.5cm)

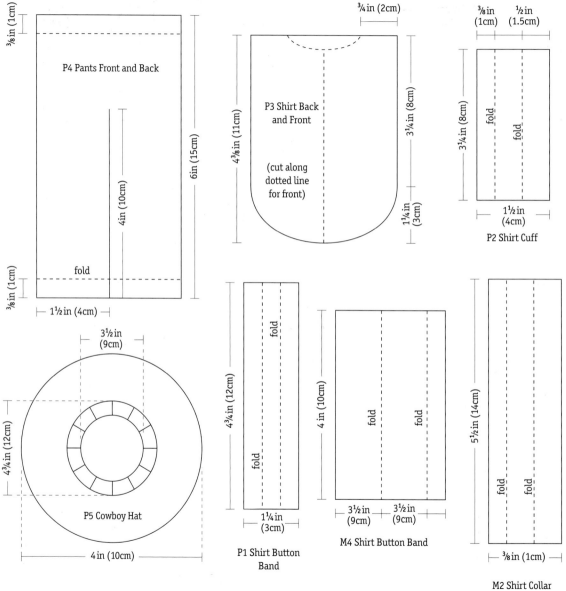

³⁄₈ in (1cm)

P4 Pants Front and Back

4in (10cm)

6in (15cm)

fold

³⁄₈ in (1cm)

1½ in (4cm)

¾ in (2cm)

P3 Shirt Back
and Front

(cut along
dotted line
for front)

4⅞ in (11cm)

3¼ in (8cm)

1¼ in (3cm)

³⁄₈ in (1cm)   ½ in (1.5cm)

fold

fold

3¼ in (8cm)

1½ in (4cm)

P2 Shirt Cuff

3½ in (9cm)

4¾ in (12cm)

4in (10cm)

P5 Cowboy Hat

fold

fold

4¾ in (12cm)

1¼ in (3cm)

P1 Shirt Button
Band

fold

fold

4 in (10cm)

3½ in (9cm)   3½ in (9cm)

M4 Shirt Button Band

fold

fold

fold

fold

5½ in (14cm)

³⁄₈ in (1cm)

M2 Shirt Collar

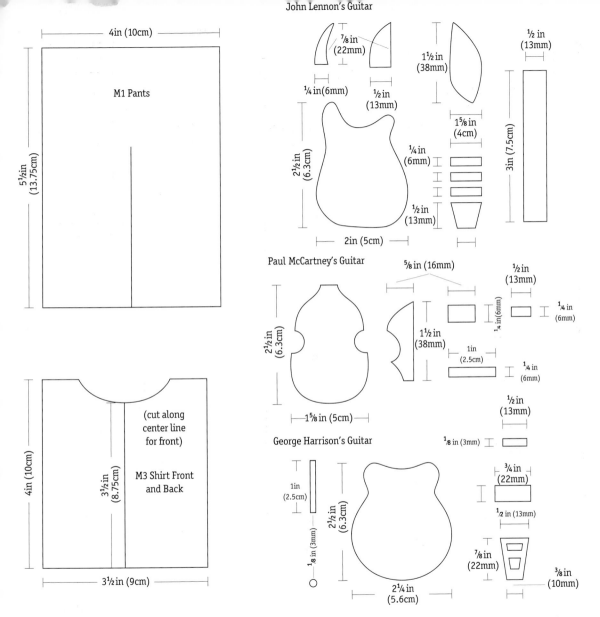

M1 Pants

4in (10cm)

5½in (13.75cm)

John Lennon's Guitar

⅞in (22mm)

¼in (6mm)

½in (13mm)

2½in (6.3cm)

2in (5cm)

1½in (38mm)

1⅝in (4cm)

¼in (6mm)

½in (13mm)

½in (13mm)

3in (7.5cm)

Paul McCartney's Guitar

⅝in (16mm)

2½in (6.3cm)

1⅝in (5cm)

1½in (38mm)

1in (2.5cm)

½in (13mm)

¼in (6mm)

¼in (6mm)

¼in (6mm)

½in (13mm)

⅛in (3mm)

George Harrison's Guitar

1in (2.5cm)

⅛in (3mm)

2½in (6.3cm)

2¼in (5.6cm)

¾in (22mm)

½in (13mm)

⅞in (22mm)

⅜in (10mm)

4in (10cm)

3½in (8.75cm)

(cut along center line for front)

M3 Shirt Front and Back

3½in (9cm)

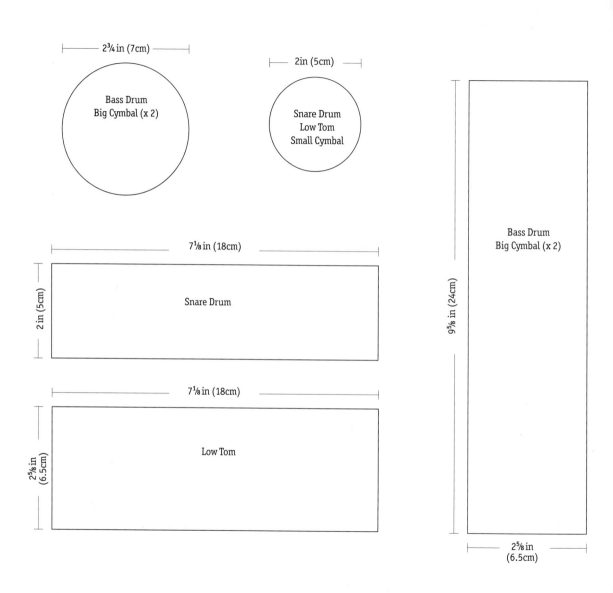

2¾ in (7cm)

Bass Drum
Big Cymbal (x 2)

2in (5cm)

Snare Drum
Low Tom
Small Cymbal

9⅝ in (24cm)

Bass Drum
Big Cymbal (x 2)

2⅝ in
(6.5cm)

7⅛ in (18cm)

2 in (5cm)

Snare Drum

7⅛ in (18cm)

2⅝ in
(6.5cm)

Low Tom

KNITTED ICONS

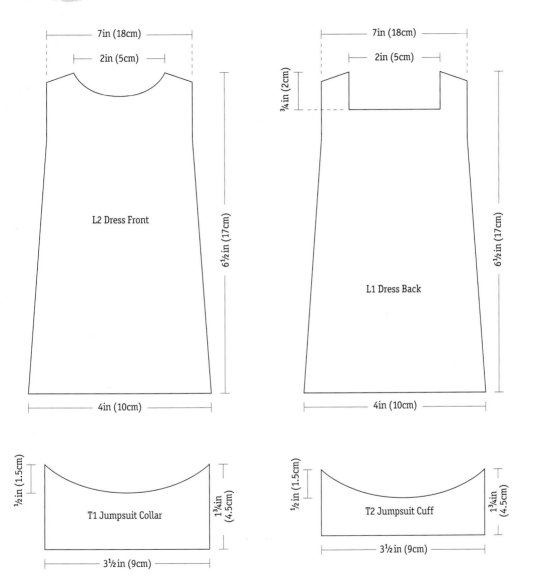

7in (18cm)

2in (5cm)

L2 Dress Front

6½in (17cm)

4in (10cm)

7in (18cm)

2in (5cm)

¾in (2cm)

L1 Dress Back

6½in (17cm)

4in (10cm)

½in (1.5cm)

T1 Jumpsuit Collar

1¾in (4.5cm)

3½in (9cm)

½in (1.5cm)

T2 Jumpsuit Cuff

1¾in (4.5cm)

3½in (9cm)

Resources

Rowan Yarns
distributed by Westminster Fibers
165 Ledge Street
Nashua, NH 03063
(603) 886-5041
www.westminsterfibers.com

Jaeger Handknits
See Rowan Yarn

Jo-Ann Stores
Locations nationwide
www.joann.com

Michael's
Locations nationwide
(800) MICHAELS
www.michaels.com

Techniques and Abbreviations

approx	approximately		MC	Main color
alt	alternate		oz	ounce(s)
beg	beginning		p	purl
cm	centimeter		p2tog	purl two together
dec	decrease		rem	remaining
in	inch(es)		psso	pass slipped stitch over
inc	increase		rep	repeat
k	knit		RH	right hand
k2tog	knit two together		RS	right side
k3tog	knit three together		sl	slip
LH	left hand		ssk	slip slip knits
m1	make one		St st	Stockinette stitch
mm	millimeter(s)		st(s)	stitch(es)
MB	Make bobble: Knit into front, back, and front of next st, turn and k3, turn and p3, turn and k3, turn and slip 1, k2tog, psso.		tbl	through back loop
			tog	together
			WS	wrong side
			yd	yard
			yfwd	yarn forward

Acknowledgments

Many thanks to Kate Buller and all the team at Rowan & Coats for the use of their gorgeous materials, yarn, and beads. Thanks also to Sandra Youngson (my Mom), Eleanor Crombie (my favorite Auntie), Jane Galbraith, and Suzanne Kirkland for helping me create the final projects. I extend my gratitude to all my friends, especially Andy for his help and encouragement throughout.

Photo Credits

4/56 iStockphoto.com/Sx70, 6 Andy Warhol Foundation/CORBIS, 18 iStockphoto.com/Nnehring, 21/73 Underwood & Underwood/CORBIS, 22 Marilyn, 24 CHINA NEWSPHOTO/Reuters/Corbis, 25 Purchased from shop, 27/84/99 John Springer Collection/CORBIS, 28 istockphoto/blackred, 32 (necklace) istockphoto.com/emily2k, 34 istockphoto.com/duncan1890, 35 Madeleine Répond/Corbis, 36 Paul Sale Vern Hoffman/Design Pics/Corbis, 37 Henry Diltz/CORBIS, 38 istockphoto.com/davo86, 40 istockphoto.com/Manfred_Konrad, 42 Douglas Kirkland/CORBIS, 43 istockphoto.com/stphilips, 46 James Dean portrait, 51 istockphoto.com/tacojim, 52 Swim Ink 2, LLC/CORBIS, 53 istockphoto.com/dononeg, 54 istockphoto.com/EddWestmacott, 55 John Springer Collection/CORBIS, 58 istockphoto.com/anzeletti, 60/95 Neal Preston/CORBIS, 61 istockphoto/stphillips, 62 True Blue, 63 Hans Gedda/Sygma/Corbis, 64-65 Andy Warhol Foundation/CORBIS, 66 istockphoto/ene, 69 Beatles, 29-32/39/41/45/47/49-50/68/70/75/76-77/89 Bettmann/CORBIS, 78 Hulton-Deutsch Collection/CORBIS, 79 iStockphoto.com/Giuseppe Pons, 81 S.I.N./CORBIS, 82 iStockphoto.com/selensergen, 83 Marley CD cover, 87 Tony Frank/Sygma/Corbis, 88 Alan Schein/zefa/Corbis, 90 istockphoto.com/sumnersgraphicsinc